PRAYER OF THE HEART

PRAYER OF THE HEART

GEORGE A. MALONEY S.J.

AVE MARIA PRESS   Notre Dame, Indiana 46556

First printing, January, 1981
Third printing, March, 1983
45,000 copies in print

Acknowledgments:

Sincere thanks to Mrs. Rita Ruggiero for typing this manuscript, to
Sister Francoise O'Hare, RSHM and Sister Joseph Agnes, SCH, for
their careful reading and correcting of the manuscript and for other
suggestions that proved most helpful. Grateful acknowledgment is
made to the following publishers: Darton, Longman & Todd, Ltd.,
and Doubleday & Company, Inc., N.Y., for excerpts from the
Jerusalem Bible, copyright 1966 by Darton, Longman & Todd,
Ltd., and Doubleday and Company, Inc. All scriptural texts are
from this Bible version unless otherwise noted.

Imprimi Potest: Rev. Vincent M. Cooke, S.J.
                 Provincial of the New York Province
                 May 1, 1980

International Standard Book Number: 0-87793-215-8 (Cloth)
                                    0-87793-216-6 (Paper)

Library of Congress Catalog Card Number: 80-69095

Printed and bound in the United States of America.

Cover and text design by Betsy Priest

*To three spiritual athletes of the
modern desert who live the prayer of the heart
in their busy lives: Kaye Tobin, Gale and Frank Tuoti.*

CONTENTS

INTRODUCTION

Once, after Socrates had described with great eloquence the ideal way human beings should live and the ideal society in which they would be able to live as perfectly as possible, his disciple, Glaucon, objected. He did not believe such a "City of God" existed anywhere on earth. Socrates answered, "Whether such a city exists in heaven or ever will exist on earth, the wise man will live after the manner of that city, having nothing to do with any other, and in so looking upon it, will set his own house in order."[1]

Most of us, living in the modern world of today, would heartily agree that our world is not quite yet that "City of God." Have you ever yielded to the temptation of thinking that perhaps in the past there was a time and a place in which you could have more easily become a fulfilled human being? Would that time be the Middle Ages when all of Europe was Christian and faith seemingly permeated all facets of human life? Or perhaps upon reading scripture, you picture yourself living in the first Christian community of Jerusalem, sharing everything in common with your brothers and sisters in Christ? Or, with a holy nostalgia, do you find yourself among the great charismatic Christians who left everything in order to build a "City of God" in the deserts of Egypt and Syria in the fourth century? Do you dream of a future time and place, on this earth or in heaven, where Utopia will finally be reached and you will be one of the chosen?

Whether you dream of the future or idealize the past, one thing is sure: You are ignoring the present situation and moment in time. St. Paul calls out to us, "Well, now is the favorable time; this is the day of salvation" (2 Cor 6:2). He tells us to wake up from our sleep (Rom 13:11) and start living lives befitting human beings and Christians. He quotes from Is 26:19 and Is 60:1:

> Wake up from your sleep,
> rise from the dead,
> and Christ will shine on you (Eph 5:14).

THE KINGDOM OF GOD IS WITHIN YOU

When Jesus began to announce the Good News of salvation, he told his listeners about the in-breaking of the heavenly Father's tender love for each individual. He called this love relationship between God and human individuals "the kingdom of God." And he himself was to make this relationship possible as individuals turned their lives over to him.

But such a new creation, a rebirth to become children of God, could come about only through a repentance, a *metanoia* or complete change of vision, of inner direction, of motivation, of values to authentic, human fulfillment and meaningfulness.

Jesus stressed in his preaching and still stresses to all of us today the importance of being vigilant, attentive, alert and awake in this present moment, for right now the kingdom of God is being accomplished among us and within us. He comes to give us abundant life (Jn 10:10), life that will never perish but will be eternal. But this, for Jesus, is not a life that awaits us hereafter in an unending series of *now* moments. Eternal life is not an infinite number but is a quality that even now is be to experienced. It is a knowledge that affects the whole person, that becomes synonymous with love.

> And eternal life is this:
> to know you,
> the only true God,
> and Jesus Christ whom you have sent (Jn 17:3).

A MEANINGFUL LIFE

Only a human person, of all God's material creatures, has the ability to stand on the mountaintop of his or her consciousness and ask the *why* and *where* of human existence. Why have I been created? Where is my life going? Where should it be going? How can I find purpose in my life? These are questions we cannot stop asking ourselves. The answers that we formulate and that guide our living determine the degree of our integration as whole and truly *alive* persons.

Jesus comes into human existence in order to set us free from the bondage that cripples us and prevents us from being integrated individuals (Lk 4:18; Jn 8:31-32). He still walks among us, establishing the kingdom of God by healing us of all our physical, psychological and spiritual sicknesses, fears, anxieties, isolation and sinful darkness (Mt 4:23-24; Mt 9:35).

We become free and healthy as whole persons to the degree that in intense consciousness of our true selves and inner awareness of our *I-ness* we freely and responsibly take our life in each moment's choices and determine to live according to the fullness of potentiality that God has put into us and into that momentary event. Through creative work done to build a better world according to the mind of God and out of love for him and our fellow neighbor, through transcendent, loving service for others, by forgetting self and living out of love to bring happiness to as many persons as we can, we grow into a life of meaningfulness.

The poet, Robinson Jeffers, shows how such "conscious" living transcends the number of years that one lives. It is dependent on rising beyond time to live eternally.

> But young or old, few years or many,
> signified less than nothing
> To him who had climbed the tower beyond
> time, consciously . . . . [2]

MEN INTOXICATED WITH GOD

In the fourth century of Christianity groups of men and women literally moved into the deserts of Egypt and Syria, and there they sought to climb "the tower beyond time, consciously." Under the power of the Spirit of Jesus Risen they stripped their lives of everything superfluous and self-centered in order to live as consciously as possible in the presence of God out of love for him who loved them infinitely in Christ Jesus.

They answered literally the call of Christ to leave all and follow him. They truly experienced the hidden treasure and were willing to sell all to obtain it. As a result their lives showed the struggle involved in this process.[3] Thomas Merton writes of their goal:

> . . . not to leave society but to transcend it; not to withdraw from the fellowship with other men, but to renounce the appearance of the myth of union in diversion in order to attain to union on a higher and more spiritual level—the level of the Mystical Body of Christ.[4]

Pseudo-Macarius in his *Spiritual Homilies* describes them as "men intoxicated with God." Impelled by the same Holy Spirit that drove Jesus into the desert, they sought to pray always, as St. Paul exhorts the Thessalonians "to pray incessantly" (1 Thes 5:17). They strove to push their mind into their "heart," the deepest level of consciousness. There, in faith, hope and love, they experienced the indwelling Trinity. There, God was establishing his kingdom. He reigned progressively more and more as the desert hermits strove vigilantly to bring every thought and imagination under captivity and into obedience to Jesus Christ (2 Cor 10:5).

These athletes of God subjected themselves to austere discipline *(ascesis)*, not because they were masochists or hated the body, but because they knew their inner dignity as children of God and temples of the Holy Spirit (1 Cor 3:16; 1 Cor 6:19). Fasting, vigils throughout the night, humble works of charity, striving to reach the inner poverty of spirit that they called humility, all such attempts were seen as means of reaching a state of integration that they referred to as *apatheia* (a passionless passion or the complete absence of selfishness in their human choices).

HESYCHASM

More positively they strove to reach a state of integration of all their body, soul and spirit relationships that they called *hesychia*. This is a Greek word that means *rest* or *tranquillity*. When such Christian warriors had conquered all bias toward themselves and Jesus became "all in all" in every conscious choice of thought, word or action, the index of the degree of their "incorporation" into Christ was measured by the love, peace and joy that they habitually experienced.

This is an Eastern Christian type of spirituality that grew out of the experiences of the desert Fathers. It is a synthesis of the Christian life centered around what Eastern Christians in general considered to be the main goal of the spiritual life: How to obey the commandments of Jesus Christ by living as consciously as possible in the loving presence of the indwelling Trinity so as to pray always. Many Westerners have understood *hesychasm* merely to refer to the psychosomatic techniques that developed in the 13th and 14th centuries on Mount Athos in the use of the Jesus Prayer. This prayer, that through the centuries became fixed with the words: "Lord, Jesus Christ, Son of God, have mercy on me, a sinner," is a mere summary of a free use of any ejaculation that served as a *mantra* to center attention upon Jesus Christ.

It would be an error to limit this hesychastic spirituality to a mere technique. It embraces, on the contrary, a summary of the entire Christian life: a patristic and biblical anthropology of God's creative and redemptive orders, sin, grace and the mysteries of the incarnation, death and resurrection of Jesus Christ, who extends his healing power through his Word and sacraments by means of his church. The most representative literary source of hesychasm is found in the *Philokalia,* a collection of the writings of the hesychastic Fathers from the fourth to the 15th centuries.

NEED FOR SPIRITUAL DIRECTION

Today a great many Western Christians are turning to the Far Eastern and Eastern Christian religions in an attempt to rediscover the element of mysticism and direct experience with God that has always been a genuine element in Christian prayer. The hesychastic Fathers were most insistent that an individual, eager for greater immanent union with God, submit himself or herself to the direction of a holy and learned spiritual director.

Deeper prayer cannot be obtained unless there is a deep, inner silence and stillness. Part of that stillness comes from stilling our mental activity and waiting humbly in deep faith that the immanently dwelling God will speak. To pass beyond the superficial levels of our controlled consciousness in order to pass into the innermost core of our being, great discipline is required. An experienced spiritual guide can help us acquire such discipline. But, above all, a director can provide the necessary prudence and discernment of spirits. As one passes through layers of psychic experiences, dangers appear. Repressed material that has been drowned in the unconscious can rise threateningly to disturb the one seeking greater union with God. Flashes and lights, psychic powers of telepathy, communing with the dead can come forth. The demonic within us can rear its many ugly heads. What is reality, what is hallucination? A guide who has done battle with the enemies of the interior world is most necessary. Psychic powers can be dangerous and evil can enter and manipulate a person seeking honestly to attain a greater oneness with God.

One aim of this book is a humble attempt to offer spiritual direction to those who have advanced somewhat beyond discursive, mental prayer and have begun to take the first steps in contemplation. Everywhere I go in America, I meet with the same question from Christians who have begun to pray scripture in a contemplative way and to find inspiration from the mystical writers of both the East and the West: "Where can I find proper spiritual direction?" This book is not a panacea for all the problems of contemplatives. It is offered as a help, especially to those who have read the *Philokalia* and are in need of an interpretation and an adaptation of the universal, Christian elements that should be found in the prayer life of all Christians, both of Western and Eastern churches.

DEMYTHOLOGIZING

Taking the classics of Christian mysticism literally or failing to transcend the cultural elements that form the backdrop of the times in which the ancient writers lived can be a source of danger to modern Christian readers. Examples can easily be seen in the writings of the Fathers of the desert who fled from society and strove to have as little contact as possible with human beings, and in the writings of St. John of the Cross. St. Isaac of Nineveh writes, "He is a monk, who stays outside the world and is ever praying to God, so that he may gain future blessings."[5] Platonism and Stoicism had become the philosophical carriers to articulate a form of Christian life for such monks of the desert. Great dangers could befall those in the 20th century who seek to imitate such a Christianity without a demythologizing attempt to sift the cultural aspects (not always very Christian!) from the truths that are always applicable in all centuries and in all cultures.

St. John of the Cross received his Christianity through the writings of St. Augustine and St. Thomas Aquinas. His spirituality was of a vertical relation between himself as an *I* relating to God as a *Thou*, heading for a mystical marriage that did not concern itself with starving millions or the threat of a nuclear destruction of the universe.

PRAYER OF THE HEART

This is also a positive book of teaching on deeper prayer. The jumping-off point will be the hesychastic spirituality as presented in the writings of the Eastern Christian writers. These writers present us with a vision of the Christian called to pray always. From Holy Scripture they work out a spirituality of awareness, of an ever-increasing consciousness of the indwelling presence of the Holy Trinity. The Old and New Testaments and the best traditions in Eastern Christianity speak of the *heart* in prayer to refer to the whole person—emotions, body, imagination, intellect and will—meeting God. Such prayer has been described by the Eastern Fathers as putting the "mind in the heart" as one prays. Such a spirituality that has as its aim a total integration of the human person as he or she meets God in prayer and learns completely to surrender to his loving presence has been called *hesychasm*. The model for the Eastern *hesychast* has always been Mary, the mother of God, as she prays, "Behold the handmaid of the Lord; be it done unto me according to thy word."

Hesychia is that state in which Christians, through grace and their own intense asceticism, reintegrate their whole being into a single *ego* that is then placed completely under the influence of God dwelling within them. Hesychia is that state of integrated *ego-hood*. It is total healing in order to become the glory of God, human beings living fully, wrote St. Irenaeus in the second century.

It is more than a contemplative form of prayer that supercedes the use of discursive powers of imagination, intellect and will, the use of words, images and feelings to communicate with God. The prayer of the heart is a way of life that is built upon a rigorous asceticism of constant control of the thoughts by vigilant attention to the presence of the indwelling God, fasting and cultivation of *penthos,* which is an abiding sense of sorrow for sin. It is an abiding state of conscious awareness of immanent union with the loving community of the indwelling Trinity combined with an equally vivid awareness of one's own individuality through the love experienced by the triune Persons. It is centered chiefly around a short prayer that becomes synchronized with the breathing and aids the pray-er to enter intimately throughout the day and night into the loving presence of Jesus.

PROCEDURE

In order, therefore, to present a book on the prayer of the heart or on how to pray constantly, I would like to follow this procedure. Each chapter will develop an essential area in spirituality of the prayer of the heart or *hesychasm*. The teaching of the Eastern Fathers who wrote about such prayer will be given. I will attempt to interpret what they were teaching by separating the limiting cultural "baggage" from the kernel of truth. Then I will give an application that will, hopefully, bring such spiritual teaching into your life in the 20th century.

Beyond any procedure, my aim in writing this book is to challenge you to enter into your "heart," into the deepest area of your consciousness and there to live your life "in Christ Jesus," a phrase that St. Paul never tires of using. This living Person dwells within you, giving you his Spirit and his power to love the Father with his own love and to love one another as he loves you. When you call upon his name incessantly, Jesus the Lord will continually reveal the Father to you. Jesus is always saying in the depths of your heart, "And I have revealed you (Father) to them and I will keep on revealing you so that the mighty love you have for me may be in them and I in them" (Jn 17:26).

My hope is that by reading this book you will experience a bit more of that amazing, almighty, tender, humble, loving Father, Son and Spirit dwelling within you, and you will be able in the recreating power of that love to go out into your modern world and love others with God's very love within you.

GEORGE A. MALONEY, S.J.

1.

HESYCHASM

We are distinguished from other animals by our inexhaustible quest for self-knowledge. We possess an inner reflective power that drives us in a relentless search for a meaningful existence. Instinct is the driving force in an animal to hunt for food, to mate and perpetuate the species and to build a dwelling place of protection from other marauding animals. But only human beings possess the intellectual and volitional faculties that allow us to ask the one question that other animals cannot ask: Why do I exist?

We can rove over the earth, conquering oceans, mountains and all conceivable natural forces. But eventually we must return to ourselves and enter within to search for the talisman that will unlock the hidden treasures of unending happiness. However, what most of us in the latter part of the 20th century experience when we do "return to ourselves" is a general spirit of *emptiness*. Dr. Rollo May describes this general malaise:

> . . . the chief problem of people in the middle decade of the twentieth century is *emptiness*. By that I mean not only that many people do not know what they want; they often do not have any clear idea of what they feel. When they talk about lack of autonomy, or lament their inability to make decisions—difficulties which are present in all decades—it soon becomes evident that their underlying problem is that they have no definite experience of their own desires or wants. Thus they feel swayed this way and that, with painful feelings of powerlessness, because they feel vacuous, empty.[1]

MEANINGLESSNESS

A universal *angst* or anxiety fills the heart of modern man with a sense of a loss of direction, of meaninglessness. Immersion in a pragmatic materialism has suffocated our communion with God deeply dwelling within our innermost self. We are adrift on a dark, stormy ocean that threatens our very meaningfulness.

Dr. Viktor E. Frankl, the Austrian psychiatrist, confirms this almost universal sense of meaninglessness that pervades modern society. He writes, "Effectively an ever-increasing number of our clients today suffer from a feeling of interior emptiness—which I have described as existential emptiness—a feeling of total absence of a meaning to existence."[2] He attributes this existential emptiness to the loss of instinct in modern man and also the loss of tradition. We no longer know what we *must* do by our instinct and we have lost the ability to know what we *ought* to do by cutting ourselves off from the roots of our past.

Conformism is the compromise for those of the Western hemisphere; totalitarianism is the common choice for those of the Eastern hemisphere. T.S. Eliot in 1925 prophetically described many who are living today:

We are the hollow men
We are the stuffed men
Leaning together
Headpiece filled with straw. Alas!
Shape without form, shade without colour,
Paralyzed force, gesture without motion.[3]

Yet there is developing among many of us a reaction that shows itself as an ardent seeking for meaningfulness as unique persons. Some seek new purpose in life in parapsychology and mind-expanding techniques. But many others are seeking answers to the question of meaningfulness in religion, whether the traditional or the new types or an eclectic gathering together of a little of each. Fundamental Protestant churches are being packed by people, even young people, eager to find in the Bible the meaning of life. Roman Catholics find among their numbers those who follow or are in sympathy with Archbishop Lefebvre or other traditionalists. The Charismatic Renewal has given hope to many who were ready to give up on a Christianity that was too static and lacked meaningfulness for daily living.

The Anglican theologian, Dr. John Macquarrie, however, sounds a much-needed alarm in regard to any new wave of enthusiasm for "religion"; ". . . especially as much of it seems to be almost entirely void of any intellectual content. Is the exuberant spirit of celebration as one-sided as the drab secularity which has provoked it? If so, it could turn out to be very dangerous."[4]

Carl G. Jung gives us his grave reservations about the wisdom of Westerners giving up their religious traditions and embracing those of the East:

> . . . my criticism is directed solely against the application of Yoga to the peoples of the West. The spiritual development of the West has been along entirely different lines from that of the East and has therefore produced conditions which are the most unfavorable soil one can think of for the application of Yoga. Western civilization is scarcely a thousand years old and must first of all free itself from its barbarous one-sidedness. This means, above all, deeper insight into the nature of man. But no insight is gained by repressing and controlling the unconscious, and least of all by imitating methods which have grown up under totally different psychological conditions. In the course of the centuries the West will produce its own Yoga and it will be on the basis laid down by Christianity.[5]

CHRISTIAN EAST

Many today are discovering part of their Christian heritage in Eastern Christianity. With enthusiasm they find basically the same doctrines as taught by the Roman Catholic Church and by many traditional Protestant churches. But what attracts such

Western Christians to the Christian East is its rich, mystical tradition. It combines in an admirable synthesis the prophetic quality found in Old Testament Judaism with the immediate, immanent experience of the indwelling Trinity that Jesus preached and made available to his followers through the Holy Spirit.

Christianity first developed in the Semitic world of Judaism. God had revealed himself to his people through his prophets. But in the Old Testament the Divine Word of God is not something abstract to be studied and reasoned over. It is primarily a transforming Word that must be experienced and have concrete repercussions upon the lives of the Christian followers. Eastern Christianity keeps alive the dynamism of the Word of God for those who hear it.

> For the word of God is quick and powerful and sharper than any two-edged sword, piercing even to the dividing asunder of soul and spirit and of the joints and marrow and is a discerner of the thoughts and intents of the heart (Heb 4:12).

As the Word of God enfleshed, Jesus Christ contains all the words of God's former revelation. He is the fullness of God made manifest among us. In this living Word "all things were created by him and for him" (Col 1:16). By his Resurrection, Jesus Christ lives within us and continues to speak God's Word to us. That preached Word spoken to the first Christian community is still being spoken in each person's existential "now" moment. In the Byzantine Liturgy of the East each day the Gospel is carried in solemn procession by the deacon or priest among the people. Then he stands in front of the people and shouts out: "Wisdom! Let us be attentive!" The faithful bow down to the Gospel as to Jesus Christ himself. Hence in the Eastern churches that sprang up from those first Christian communities of Jerusalem and Antioch and Alexandria, the Word of God is central to the communal liturgical prayer as well as the individual Christian's prayer life. God is still speaking his same Word to those who have the ears to hear.

DIVINE IMMANENCE

Christianity added a revolutionary element of divine immanence within man that could never have been dreamt of by the non-Christian religions. This was not to be an assimilation whereby we would lose our identity as human beings. Rather, we would experience our true identity in loving submission to the triadic uncreated energies of God abiding within us. Jesus Christ teaches that, as a result of living according to the Word of God, we have a new immanent relation to the indwelling, triune God. "If anyone love me, he will keep my word and my Father will love him and we will come to him and make our abode with him" (Jn 14:23).

Christian prayer allows us, by the Holy Spirit's gift of faith, to enter into a continued living experience of being "begotten" by the Father in the Word through the Holy Spirit. Thus Christianity, as it evolved in the East, would mingle in a healthy synthesis the two basic polarities of God without and God within. The synthesis that best characterizes Eastern Christian spirituality has been called *hesychasm*.

AN EVOLVING SPIRITUALITY

Hesychasm is a Christian form of living the spiritual life that has it roots in the first hermits who fled into the barren deserts of Egypt and Syria during the fourth century. One author defines hesychasm as a spiritual system of essentially contemplative orientation which finds the perfection of man in union with God through continuous prayer.[6] However it is defined, hesychasm must not be limited solely to the mechanical recitation of the Jesus Prayer, along with the technique of respiration, sitting posture and fixation on the navel. It is true that in the 14th century a renaissance of hesychasm on Mount Athos did focus attention on such techniques, but the essential features of this spirituality developed much earlier and were conceived of as an entire way of life in Christ designed for totally committed Christians striving in the physical deserts to be completely focused in loving surrender upon the indwelling Trinity. From such a desert spirituality hesychasm evolved as it received various influences from spiritual writers representing the Antiochene and Alexandrian schools of thought.

HESYCHIA

The desert hermits, who form the beginnings of this spirituality, were merely seeking to flee from the multiplicity of their lives by living in the desert as simply as possible and devoting most of their waking hours to incessant prayer. St. Arsenius the Great has always been considered an example of the perfect hesychast, the Christian who silenced his heart in order to listen to God's Word speak within. Hesychast comes from the Greek word *hesychia* which means tranquillity or peace. Hesychia is that state in which the Christian through grace and his own intense asceticism reintegrates his whole being into a single person that is then placed completely under the direct influence of the Trinity dwelling within him.

Arsenius, as the story is told in the *Lives of the Fathers*, while still at the imperial court of Constantinople, prayed to God in these words, "Lord, lead me along a way of life where I can be saved." A voice said to him, "Arsenius, flee men and you will be saved." The same Arsenius, now a hermit in the desert, made again his same prayer and heard a voice which said to him, "Arsenius, flee, keep silence, remain tranquil; these are the roots of impeccability."[7]

This formed the basis for the hesychastic spirituality. The first stage consisted in a "fleeing from men" that was spatial, external and physical. Such a separation from society was not an end in itself and certainly was not encouraged because of a belief that society was totally evil. It was considered a means to a higher end: attaining the most intimate union with God. To attain this state of awareness of living in the presence of God day and night, the hermits knew that they had to flee from noise by exterior and interior silence, which, in the words of St. Basil, is the beginning of purity of the heart.[8] St. John Climacus further defines silence: first of all as detachment from concern with regard to necessary and unnecessary things; second, as assiduous prayer; and third, as the unremitting action of prayer in the heart.[9]

Thus such physical withdrawal was only a means to attain a spiritual state of inner silence, of attention to the presence of God within. Again St. John Climacus shows us the relationship of physical withdrawal to the withdrawal from all obstacles to inner integration, "Close the door of your cell physically, the door of your tongue to speech and the inward door to the evil spirits."[10] The true journey of the hesychast is not merely a physical journey into the desert or away from society; its essence consists in the inward journey into the "heart." The hesychast has meditated on the words of the Lord, "The kingdom of God is within you" (Lk 17:21). And so he seeks his true self by listening to the Word of God that resides within his heart.

Such desert athletes knew from their own reflective experience that, in order to listen to the indwelling Word of God, they had to give up all attention to themselves. The demands of self-love had to be silenced so that God could communicate his loving presence to them. The heart had to be quiet. This silencing of the heart and bringing it to full attention to God's inner operations was the goal of *praxis*, the austere regime of ascetical practices that aimed at breaking the dominance of the false self. All practices of vigils, fasting, solitude and silence had meaning only to develop *hesychia* or inner tranquillity of the heart.

THE HEART

The heart in scriptural language is the seat of human life, of all that touches us in the depths of our personality: all affections, passions, desires, knowledge and thoughts. It is in our "heart" that we meet God in an I-Thou relationship.[11] The heart, therefore, in scriptural language and as used by the hesychastic writers, is the center of our being, that which directs us in our ultimate values and choices. It is the inner chamber where in secret the heavenly Father sees us through and through. It is where we attain inner honesty, integration and "purity of heart."

St. Theophan the Recluse (1815-1894), one of the outstanding 19th-century Russian mystics, describes the heart in the hesychastic tradition:

> The heart is the innermost man or spirit. Here are located self-awareness, the conscience, the idea of God and of one's complete dependence on Him, and all the eternal treasures of the spiritual life. . . . Where is the heart? Where sadness, joy, anger, and other emotions are felt, here is the heart. Stand there with attention. . . . Stand in the heart, with the faith that God is also there, but how He is there do not speculate. Pray and entreat that in due time love for God may stir within you by His grace. [12]

How can we understand such a symbol as that of the *heart* to mean our deepest levels of consciousness and inner awareness, as the "place" where we meet God? Because of our "being-in-the-world," we are basically creatures who are not naturally, all the time, focused upon God in consciousness that he is our beginning and our end. We are being pulled in all directions by persons, things and events that clamor for our attention. We need to have a "focus"[13] in order that our deepest relationship with God in an intimate, personal, loving union may not be too diffuse and abstract. We need a concrete presence in which our loving relationship with God may command the center of our consciousness and awareness and thus exert maximum influence on our thoughts, words and actions.

Our human heart is both a physical organ and a basic symbol of our existence in life. Even more, the heart symbolizes our transcendence beyond the world, the inner stretching power within our spirit to go toward God in thought and love. We are commanded to love God with our whole heart, our whole mind, our whole strength (Dt 6:6). Yahweh speaks through the prophet Jeremiah, "When you seek me you shall find me, when you seek me with all your heart" (Jer 29:13). The writers of Holy

Scripture were using a powerful symbol as a point from which, while still rooted in this world, the heart could swing free, moving into the fullness for which it was created, namely, to embrace God in the loving relationship of child to Father. The Fathers of the desert were only being scriptural when they used the heart as the place where we encounter God with all our strengths, but also with all our brokenness and sinfulness that cry out for healing from God. It referred in their thinking also to the "new creation" or, in Pauline terms, "the new man" that was healed, integrated and transformed into a new creature in Christ Jesus (2 Cor 5:17).

A HEART SPIRITUALITY

Pseudo-Macarius, who wrote his *Fifty Spiritual Homilies* in the latter part of the fourth century,[14] is one of the main influences in hesychasm of the heart spirituality. He continues the more Semitic influence with its accent on the total, existential encounter with God in the "heart" found chiefly in the Antiochene School of St. Ignatius of Antioch, Polycarp, Irenaeus and Antony of the desert. God is encountered as the ground of one's being, primarily in the heart and not in the mind. Macarius insists on the total encountering in ever-increasing awareness and even "feeling" of that presence of the indwelling Trinity. He describes in his 15th homily the mythic use of heart as the focus where God meets man in his concrete existence. The divinizing effect of the Holy Spirit works through grace to lead man into ever-mounting levels of transcendent possibility and realized human development according to the Image and Likeness that is Jesus Christ:

> His (God's) very grace writes in their hearts the laws of the Spirit. They, therefore, should not put all their trusting hope solely in the scriptures written in ink. For, indeed, divine grace writes on the "tables of the heart" (2 Cor 3:3) the laws of the Spirit and the heavenly mysteries. For the heart directs and governs all the other organs of the body. And when grace

pastures the heart, it rules over all the members and the thoughts. For there in the heart the mind abides as well as all the thoughts of the soul and all its hopes. This is how grace penetrates throughout all parts of the body.[15]

Besides the essential elements stressed in all spiritualities of early Christianity, such as the emphasis placed on incessant prayer, free will and the cohabitation of sin and grace in man and the need to be rooted in Holy Scripture, Macarius and those who followed him put a unique stress on the centrality of Jesus Christ and the "feeling" of grace which he calls "the baptism in the Holy Spirit." That grace, through *penthos* (an abiding sorrow for sins), leads the Christian to ever-increasing levels of conscious awareness of oneness with Jesus.

AN INTELLECTUAL SPIRITUALITY

The heart spirituality of Macarius is in contrast to the intellectual emphasis given to hesychastic spirituality by Origen and Evagrius and those writers who followed their teachings. It is especially Evagrius (+ 399) who articulates for the monks of the desert a spirituality that borrows from the metaphysics and anthropology of Neoplatonism. If we are to understand hesychasm and to seek to demythologize it of the particular cultural aspects that no longer seem applicable, we must look especially at the influence of Evagrius. His two works in particular, *Praktikos* and *Chapters on Prayer*,[16] bequeathed to hesychastic spirituality a vocabulary and a vision of the spiritual life that still exercise a great influence on Eastern Christian piety, especially on monasticism.

The world view of Evagrius is based on that of Origen and has come down to us in the writings of Cassian, especially his *Institutes* and *Conferences*, which are perhaps the writings most responsible for this philosophy which lies behind medieval monasticism of both East and West. Even modern religious life is rooted in this vision. It presents a primitive, spiritual cosmos, paradisiacal in its harmony, which, however, fell with man's sin into a state of limitation or captivity. Matter has an intimate connection with this fallen condition of the cosmos. Man's primitive state, which he is ever bent on attaining again, was a pure contemplation of the Trinity with an intellect naked of all forms. Man fell into an attachment to multiplied forms and to a love of sensible objects for their own sakes.

In this vision demons play an important role as man's entire life on earth consists of a constant struggle against them. Hence the spiritual life is entered first of all in the *praxis* or the ascetical practices. These consist in resisting the subtle temptations (the *logismoi*) of the evil spirits and in striving to spiritualize matter in an attempt to return to union with God through a *gnosis* or contemplative knowledge. This spiritualization of man's knowledge of created things is called *theoria physike*. The monk, through purification of the passions of the body and the mind, attains a state of passionlessness *(apatheia)* or great, inner sensitivity to the presence of God. This presence of God reveals itself in an intuitive grasp of the *Logos* or mind of God found in the things of nature. But even this level of contemplation must be further spiritualized of all material forms so that man, like the angels, may be led into the primitive state of his former existence and contemplate the Trinity without forms and images.

Prayer for Evagrius is the greatest means of cooperating with the will of God and entering from *gnosis* to a state of uninterrupted union with God called *agape* or pure love. True or pure prayer is mysticism that Evagrius equates with true theology. In an often quoted text of Evagrius we read: "If you are a theologian you truly pray. If you truly pray you are a theologian."[17]

The ideal for the contemplative, according to Evagrius, is to move through purification away from any multiplied forms, where the root of attachment and hence sin lies, and to enter into an angelic state of union with God without images. He describes this:

When your spirit withdraws, as it were, little by little from the flesh because of your ardent longing for God, and turns away from every thought that derives from sensibility or memory or temperament and is filled with reverence and joy at the same time, then you can be sure that you are drawing near that country whose name is prayer.[18]

Such a state of prayer with no distractions is called the state of "pure prayer." Undistracted prayer is an illumination given as a gift from God. It follows, but is not caused by, man's efforts to purify himself. Still we must keep in mind that this state of illumination is not a mere matter of purifying the intellect by emptying it of all images. It is God himself who purifies the human intelligence. He does this not only by means of *gnosis* (knowledge) but also by *agape* (love). The contemplative monk does not see God directly by his own light, which for Evagrius would mean an impossible share in the beatific vision, but he is seen in the naked and light-filled intellect which mirrors God as a pure and perfect image. This pure intellect is the place where God and man meet in love, the *locus Dei*.

AN INNER LIGHT

The contemplative beholds God as in a mirror, in the light of man's nature as essentially spirit (the primitive state of man). Seeing his true "self" in a state of complete purity and "nakedness," the person of contemplative prayer discovers God as the author and ground of the "self." Thus the highest contemplation does not involve two acts but only one. The basis for this understanding of the contemplative act is the biblical doctrine of the image of God in man. The "first" contemplation *(theoria physike)* attains God through inferior objects which bear the imprint of his wisdom, while the "second" *(theoria theologike)* possesses him in the spirit, the likeness of his very Being.

Usually Evagrius resorts to apophatic expressions to indicate that such knowledge cannot be comprehended by any rational concept. But he does use a very important expression that was later to be developed by such hesychastic authors as St. Symeon the New Theologian and St. Gregory Palamas. In such a degree of pure prayer, man, the purified spirit, "begins to see its own light."[19]

He also uses an important phrase that would foster the concept of "hesychia" or the attainment of inner calm. In such formless prayer, purified of all passion and emptied of all images and concepts, the spirit is then able to "remain in its own deep calm."[20] In both of these phrases used by Evagrius what is stressed is that it is a "natural" condition of the human spirit both to see God in its own light and in doing so to teach it the fullness of integration that registers deep peace, calm, inner harmony and tranquillity. Both of these elements of inner light and inner calm became central elements of hesychasm.

THE NAME OF JESUS

Thus we see at the end of the fourth century two distinct Eastern Christian spiritualities, distinct by their diverse points of emphasis: that of Macarius and that of Evagrius. Diadochus of Photice in Epirus (fifth century) did much to bring these two currents of spirituality together into a more consistent biblical spirituality. He skillfully combined the following elements: the philosophical background of Evagrius, the Macarian emphasis on the spiritualization of the individual Christian, the biblical stress on the essential doctrine concerning the fall of humankind, the centrality of the redemption of Jesus Christ, and the promise of the transformation of man and his universe in the life to come.[21]

But the center of hesychasm, beginning in the sixth century and continuing over several centuries, was the Monastery of St. Catherine on Mount Sinai. Here the true synthesis of the best of these two currents of spirituality took place. Symbolically, in the beautiful mosaic icon in the apse of the church, the transfiguration of Moses in the darkness of the cloud of unknowing on Mount Sinai and his sharing in the transfiguration of Jesus on Mount Tabor in his Taboric light is commemorated. This Sinaite school of hesychastic spirituality is represented chiefly by Nilus, John Climacus, Hesychius and Philotheus.

With their emphasis on the solitary life, on "guarding of the heart," and on mental prayer, they transmitted from Evagrius the synthesis he made of Origen and the Fathers of the desert. The Fathers stressed the hesychasm of ascetical practices designed to develop *hesychia* or tranquillity, both exterior and interior. This meant emphasizing flight from the society of other men and women, and silence of lips and heart by reducing all cares to only the absolute essential one, the evangelical occupation of seeking the kingdom of God. This interior struggle to live only for God was carried on by a constant vigilance or sobriety over one's thoughts. When, through inner attention, the mind or heart attained *hesychia* or rest from passionate thoughts, it was able to contemplate God unceasingly.[22]

To this *praxis* the teaching of Evagrius on contemplation or *theoria* is added. Thus the mind, the mirror of God, now purified, is able to contemplate unceasingly the Trinity through its own divinization through grace. Man's spirit becomes a temple of God and *apatheia*, the state of integration without the passions being a burden or impediment to prayer, brings about continual prayer or contemplation of God.

The Sinaite school combines this with the Macarian emphasis. Man is no longer as Evagrius described him, an "intellect," but man now is a *heart*. He encounters God totally in an I-Thou loving relationship, not through images. Even corporeal visions are to be discredited and the presence of God is to be guarded in the heart by *penthos* (abiding sorrow for one's sins), which is developed by the continual thought of death and judgment, the gift of tears and complete detachment from all creatures. Yet a new element is found in the Sinaite form of hesychasm and that is the personal, warm devotion to Jesus which is brought about by a simple ejaculation or merely the name of Jesus, repeated indefinitely as the form of centering in the consciousness (the *heart*) upon the transforming presence of the healing Jesus.

The most famous of all the Sinaite Fathers is undoubtedly St. John Climacus (so called because he wrote the classic: *The Ladder* (in Greek *klimax*) *of Paradise*.[23] We find much of Evagrius' spirituality in his writing. Posterity would take from John Climacus his remembrance of God's presence by the use of a short phrase repeated often, usually connected with the name or salvific function of Jesus, and always stressing the cry for mercy and forgiveness. One of his famous texts reads:

> Let the thought of death keep you company when you go to sleep and when you wake up, and with it the one-word prayer of Jesus *(monologistos Jesou euche)*. For nothing can come to you in sleep which is able to prevail over such protection.[24]

At this time of development of hesychasm there was not yet the fixed formulation of the Jesus Prayer, "Lord, Jesus Christ, Son of God, have mercy on me, a sinner." According to I. Hausherr, Climacus advocated what the earlier desert Fathers had taught in stressing the "hidden work" (in Greek *krypte ergasia*). This meant the main work of the Fathers was to recall the memory of God or the presence of God at all waking times through the utterance, vocally or mentally, of a short phrase.[25] This is brought out in Climacus' statement defining hesychia:

> Hesychia is continual adoration of the ever-present God. Let the memory of Jesus be united to your breath and then you will know the benefit of hesychia . . . the downfall of a hesychast is interrupting prayer.[26]

One final text that would have great influence in linking hesychasm with the repetition of the name of Jesus is Climacus' statement, "Whip your enemies with the name of Jesus, for there is no weapon more powerful in heaven or on earth."[27] Here Climacus uses the name of Jesus in the Semitic sense of *presence*. Later generations of hesychasts, reading these texts of

Climacus, would be led literally to use the name of Jesus as a Christian "mantra" in order to thwart the attacks of the demons and call down the mercy of the Lord.

Philotheus of Sinai, a disciple of Climacus, brings Byzantine hesychasm a step closer to a constant repetition of the name of Jesus:

> Sweet memory of God, that is, Jesus, coupled with heartfelt wrath and beneficent contrition, can always annihilate all the fascination of thoughts, the variety of suggestions . . . daringly seeking to devour our souls. Jesus when invoked easily burns up all this. For in no other place can we find salvation except in Jesus Christ. . . . And so every hour and every moment let us zealously guard our heart from thoughts obscuring the mirror of the soul, which should contain, drawn and imprinted on it, only the radiant image of Jesus Christ, who is the wisdom and the power of God the Father.[28]

THE JESUS PRAYER

Through the influence of such men as Diadochus, John Climacus, Philotheus and Hesychius of Mount Sinai, the rather wide freedom granted hesychasts in reciting an ejaculation as a centering technique upon the presence of Jesus Christ began to be restricted to a fixed formula: "Lord, Jesus Christ, Son of God, have mercy upon me, a sinner." This is seen in a document accredited falsely to St. John Chrysostom. The text reads:

> I implore you, brethren, never to abandon the rule of prayer or neglect it. . . . Eating and drinking, at home or on a journey or whatever he does, a monk should constantly call: "Lord Jesus Christ, Son of God, have mercy upon me." This remembering of the name of our Lord Jesus Christ should incite him to battle with the enemy. By this remembrance a soul forcing itself to this practice can discover everything which is within, both good and bad. . . . The name of our Lord Jesus Christ, descending into the depths of the heart, will subdue the serpent holding sway over the pastures of the heart and will save our soul and bring it to

life. Thus abide constantly with the name of our Lord Jesus
Christ, so that the heart swallows the Lord and the Lord the heart
and the two become one. But this work is not done in one or two
days; it needs many years and a long time. For great and pro-
longed labor is needed to cast out the foe so that Christ dwells in
us.[29]

Here we see that the former freedom and spontaneity in a
monk's choice of a formula to be repeated incessantly are replaced with an exact prayer and no other. This document appears to be of a later date than the 12th-century writings of
Nicephorus. To Nicephorus, according to the research of I.
Hausherr, is credited the writing of the treatise, *On the Three
Methods of Attention and Prayer*.[30] This document, more than
any other in the history of hesychasm, tied the ancient traditions
of the Fathers of the desert in their vigilant attempts to attain
inner awareness and sobriety *(nepsis)* to physio-psychological
techniques that seemingly often reflect a Muslim influence with
its use of the *dhikr* or sacred name of Allah.[31]

RENAISSANCE OF MOUNT ATHOS

It is St. Gregory of Sinai who must be credited with having
started a renaissance of hesychasm on Mount Athos in the 14th
century. He is known as the teacher of holy sobriety and of the
active method of the prayer of the mind-in-the-heart. In his
Texts on Commandments and Dogmas we find traditional,
solid teaching of the Sinaite Fathers on asceticism and prayer.
But in his *Instruction to Hesychasts* he sets down in exact detail
instructions on how to sit in one's cell, how to say the Jesus
Prayer, how to drive away thoughts, how to breathe and divide
the Jesus Prayer in order to synchronize it with one's
breathing.[32]

Gregory brought the teachings of the hesychastic Fathers to
the peninsula of Mount Athos and started a movement that was
to establish hesychasm as the central mystical doctrine of Orthodoxy.[33] He insists on the purification of the soul and the

struggle against the passions, on the necessity of arriving at Evagrius' *apatheia,* the infusion of divine light and supernatural knowledge of the created world with intimate union of the soul with God, as his predecessors, especially Climacus and Symeon the New Theologian taught. He hands down quite faithfully the ascetical purification of the "heart" of his Sinaite predecessors and builds up the tendency of Symeon to concretize and localize the supernatural experience in man's heart. Thus we have the Jesus Prayer, "Lord, Jesus Christ, Son of God, have mercy on me, a sinner," linked with the rhythm of controlled breathing. This was not only an oral prayer, but it was to be spontaneously aligned with the heart's beating so that, through it, thoughts would be controlled and the heart would "pray always" as St. Paul enjoins the early Christians.

Through constant prayer the way was opened to the contemplation of God. To attain a spontaneous "prayer of the heart," St. Gregory specifies in detail the position of the body so it will facilitate slow breathing and aid the soul in entering the heart. But over and over again Gregory insists on the great danger of self-deception and the necessity of listening to spiritual guides rather than following one's own inclinations. All in all, he emphasizes, more than any single element in the material technique of performing the Jesus Prayer, the necessity of accompanying prayer with such virtues as fasting, abstinence, vigil, patience, courage, silence, tears and humility, all virtues greatly stressed by the early Fathers of the desert.

A canon of the approved hesychastic Fathers was drawn together in the writings of Patriarch Callistus and Ignatius of Xanthopoulos in their *Directions to Hesychasts in a Hundred Chapters (Century).*[34] In this writing the two hesychastic tendencies are melded together for all time. The first is the intellectual, contemplative tendency of Evagrius, Diadochus, Maximus and the Sinaite Fathers, stressing control of all thoughts through solitude, sobriety and weeping for sins so that the mind, freed from influence of the passions, can contemplate God within. The other tendency stresses the constant repetition of the Jesus Prayer with its material techniques of breathing, posture and the Taboric light as an experience visible to the corporeal eyes.

UNCREATED ENERGIES

It was St. Gregory Palamas (+ 1359) who came to the defense of the hesychastic Fathers against the polemical attacks of the Italian Greek monk, Barlaam of Calabria.[35] Barlaam lampooned the reported experiences of the monks of Mount Athos who, using the Jesus Prayer, claimed to experience God in experiencing the Taboric light. Gregory Palamas distinguished between the essence of God, that no human person could ever totally experience, and the uncreated energies of God's love that are available to mystical experience to persons of deep contemplative prayer. These energies are not accidents or things. They are, according to Gregory, God in his triune, energetic relationships toward his created world. The end of these energies is to divinize man into a sharer of God's very own nature by grace.

Although Gregory adds nothing new to the hesychastic method as such, his name is associated with the final form that hesychasm took.[36] In his treatise *On the Blessed Hesychasts*[37] Gregory Palamas gives a defense of the method and places it in its true, subservient relation with the essence of hesychasm. His writings would prove to be the canonization of the hesychast spirituality for Orthodoxy in its claim not only to have been always the true, traditional spirituality of the Christian, Byzantine Orient, but to the only spirituality for future Orthodox generations. Through sobriety and self-mastery, the mind must be held within the body so that the whole person can partake of the greatness of the mind. But how can the mind be controlled unless it be collected and confined within the body and not be allowed to be dispersed into multiplicity through the senses? By returning into oneself, man is permitted to ascend to God.

The writings of the traditional hesychastic Fathers, including Gregory Palamas, were assembled into what has come down to us under the term of *Philokalia* (in Greek, meaning "the love of the good"). This was compiled by Macarius of Corinth (+1805) and Nicodemus Hagiorite (+1809) and first published in Greek in Venice in 1782. It was partially translated into Church Slavonic by Paissy Velitchkovsky (1722-1794). Paissy started a hesychastic renaissance in Rumania where he was abbot of the Neamt Monastery. This renaissance spread throughout all of the Slavic world, especially into Russia. The hesychastic spirituality had earlier come to Russia through the writings of St. Nil Sorsky (+1508) who had lived on Mount Athos and formed in northern Russia a cadre of deeply contemplative and ascetic monks who perpetuated the best of the teachings of the earlier hesychastic Fathers.[38]

At the end of the 19th century Theophan the Recluse made a translation of the *Philokalia* that included more hesychastic writers than the translation of Paissy. He called it by the same name as that used by Paissy, *Dobrotoliubie* but Theophan was careful to drop out any part of the *Philokalia* that stressed too heavily the physical techniques, for both he and Bishop Ignatius Brianchaninov (1807-1867) were aware of abuses brought about by the use of such techniques without proper spiritual direction.[39] But without a doubt the one work that popularized the Jesus Prayer and brought it within easy reach and practice for the laity of Russia and through the Russian immigrants to Westerners was the small, anonymous work entitled, *The Way of the Pilgrim*.[40]

The Way of the Pilgrim is a delightful tale of a Russian peasant who walks on foot through Russia, especially through Siberia, while he prays the Jesus Prayer. Here is a spirituality open to the most ordinary person who would discipline himself to enter into his "heart" and there experience the inner light of the indwelling Jesus. The Pilgrim tells his readers:

> And that can be done by anyone. It costs nothing but the effort to sink down in silence into the depths of one's heart and call more and more upon the radiant Name of Jesus. Everyone who

does that feels at once the inward light, everything becomes understandable to him, he even catches sight in this light of some of the mysteries of the Kingdom of God. And what depth and light there is in the mystery of a man coming to know he has this power to plumb the depths of his own being, to see himself from within, to find delight in self-knowledge, to take pity on himself and shed tears of gladness over his fall and his spoiled will![41]

The way in which hesychasm has come to the West has been, therefore, mainly through the popular use of the Jesus Prayer. This prayer is short and instructions given in the *Philokalia* or *The Way of the Pilgrim* show how easy it is to synchronize the prayer, made up of the transcendence of the Lord Jesus Christ and man's own sinfulnesss, with one's breathing. If anyone seeks to follow in detail the instructions found in the *Philokalia*, he will find techniques to help his concentration of mind such as physical immobility, control or suspension of breathing, fixation of the eyes on the area of the physical heart, stomach or navel in order to "push the mind into the heart," a phrase common in the writings of the hesychastic Fathers. The delights of such mysticism are painted in feelings of an inner warmth and a physical perception of the inner light called the "Taboric light."

TRUE HESYCHASM

This chapter has presented a cursory, historical view of hesychastic spirituality. We see that it has its origins in the Gospel and the spirituality of the men and women who fled into the deserts of Egypt, Syria and Palestine in the fourth and fifth centuries. But it is far from being a monolithic spirituality, consistently founded on static elements that have been passed from generation to generation, without any change or addition.

Macarius, rooted in a Semitic, Syrian spirituality of the "heart" added the holistic element of incessant prayer of the whole person through body-soul-spirit relationships. This accent highlighted the "feeling" consciousness of the presence of Jesus dwelling within the "heart," the deepest level or "focus" of awareness of an individual human person as he or she encounters God as the Ground of human being.

Evagrius and his Neoplatonic intellectualism stressed the emptying of the mind of all images and thoughts so as to reach the passionless state of oneness with God. The soul "returned" to its true nature as a mirror reflecting the ever-present Light of God.

Ascetical practices, rooted in scripture, but also inspired greatly by the philosophy of man as propounded by Stoicism and Neoplatonism, were always an essential element in hesychasm. Part of the asceticism deemed necessary to bring the Christian into a total listening and surrendering of self to the indwelling Trinity was the discipline of centering upon the repetition of the Jesus Prayer while synchronizing its mental recitation with the breathing.

This has been a cursory review of the historical developments of Byzantine hesychasm. In the remaining chapters we will concentrate on particular elements, essential to this type of Eastern Christian spirituality.

It was Rudolph Bultmann who took Martin Heidegger's existential analysis of man's inauthentic and authentic being as his hermeneutical principle and used it to "demythologize" the myths that he discovered in Holy Scripture. Can we not take the spirituality of the hesychastic Fathers and "demythologize" the mythopoetic language that they used in order to purify their message? It will be the aim of each chapter, not only to interpret what the Fathers were teaching of authentic Christianity, but also to adapt such elements into an authentic spirituality for modern Christians.

2.

FLIGHT INTO SILENT SOLITUDE

God has implanted in all of us a fiery desire to preserve our life. In the face of any threat to a secure possession of our life, we will either resort to *fight* or *flight*. Fear has the positive aspect of being a defensive mechanism. It is an instinctive way of functioning in order to maintain the security of what we treasure, our very own life.

One characteristic of not only the hesychastic Fathers but of all Christian and even non-Christian mystics throughout all the ages is the strong accent placed on running away from the "world." Jesus predicted that the "world" would hate his followers just as it hated him (Jn 17:14).

The New Testament attitude toward the "world" was one of indifference. The attitude of the early Christians, men and women who fled from the world as from a fearful enemy, was one of definite protest. Emperor Constantine put an end to the era of martyrdom and embraced the church as the official religion of the Roman Empire. But Jesus' message was very quickly distorted. A. Whitehead writes:

> When the Western world accepted Christianity, Caesar conquered. . . . The Church gave unto God the attributes which belonged exclusively to Caesar.[1]

The church and state wedded into a *symphonia*, with the church accommodating itself and its message to the wishes of the state. It no longer actively opposed the "worldliness" that in earlier centuries was seen as the most immediate enemy of Christianity. St. Basil writes of the state of Christianity in the fourth century:

The doctrines of the Fathers are despised, the speculations of in-
novators hold sway in the church. Men are rather contrivers of
cunning systems than theologians. The wisdom of this world has
the place of honor, having dispossessed the boasting of the cross.
The shepherds are driven out; in their place grievous wolves are
brought in which harry the flock. Houses of prayer have none to
assemble in them; the deserts are full of mourners.[2]

FLIGHT INTO THE DESERT

A strange movement of protest developed among serious-
minded Christians who fled into the deserts of Egypt, Syria and
Mesopotamia. Prior to Constantine's edict of toleration, the
pagan world fought to eliminate the Christian by martyrdom.
Now it is the hermit who takes up the attack and eliminates the
world from his being. The dominant tone is aggression. The
darkened prisons where Christians wasted away, the am-
phitheaters where voracious beasts tore the martyrs apart were
replaced by the immense, hot and arid desert. For these early
athletes of Christ, the desert was the twilight zone between the
profane world that groaned under the bondage of sin or chaotic
disorientation from God and the heavenly Jerusalem of the
transfigured world to come.

They did not run away from the world in cowardliness or in
self-centered spiritual egoism, but, rather, as conscious co-
creators, fighters at the most advanced outposts, "men intoxicated with God," as Macarius called them. They were
eschatological prophets, building a community, a way of life
with God that most closely would resemble the life to come in
the *eschaton*. Though living in a body in time and space, they
pointed to a transfigured, spiritual existence outside of time and
space. We are told by Palladius in his *Lausaic History* that
thousands of men and women left the cities to build large communities according to St. Paul's "New Creation," throughout
all of Egypt, Syria and Mesopotamia.

The Fathers of the desert were preparing for the development of a Christian-cultured society. Corporate mankind could not encounter God by starting from fallen nature, from people infected with an autonomous self-centeredness and a basic refusal to open themselves to God as their supreme reality. God remains exterior to the individual as well as to society in the pro-portion that the passions are interior and self-possessive. Paradoxically, the ascent toward God begins with a descent into oneself. Man, as the Fathers of the desert knew, must break through the initial fear of leaving his world of sense and psychic experiences that so easily assure him of his own self-sufficiency in order to descend into his true ego.

The arid and burning desert flourished as a "spiritual meadow." The goal of these ascetics was to "recapitulate all things in Christ," as St. Paul writes (2 Cor. 5:19; Col 1:20), to return to the state of the first man. By entering their true *self* in God they would fructify the seeds of divinity placed in them when God decreed to make man according to his own image and likeness (Gn 1:26). St. Macarius in his second homily writes:

> When, indeed, the Apostle says: "Put off the old man" (Eph 4:22), he refers to the entire man, having new eyes in place of the old, ears replacing ears, hands for hands, feet for feet.[3]

Not only did the Fathers of the desert protest against the diluted form of Christianity that resulted in its accommodating its message to the worldliness of the court of Constantinople, but they were a "remnant" people in the desert, calling Chris-tians back to the true message of Jesus Christ. We might think that the fierceness of their ascetical practices—vigils, fastings, mortifications, constant prayer—is an exaggeration, perhaps even not so much a virtue as a vice. Our common sense tells us that God does not ask so much of us; yet the spirituality of the desert shouts out to us the terrible jealousy of God who, after giving himself, asks all from his children. The Fathers of the desert had met God person to person. They responded to his condescending love to men by a total gift of themselves. Their example points out to us the ideal of Christianity, "Thou shalt love the Lord thy God with thy whole heart, with thy whole mind, with all thy strength.''

AN INTERPRETATION

With their emphasis on flight from the world and observances of complete silence and solitude, abuses did creep in and perpetuate themselves in the spirituality of later centuries. The *Imitation of Christ* praised as an ideal the saying, ''As oft as I have been among men, I returned home less a man than I was before.''[4]

The ''flesh'' of the New Testament, especially as St. Paul so often used it (*sarx* in Greek), was all too often made synonymous with the human body. To beat the body into submission by terrifying fasts, vigils and self-inflicted punishments all too often became a stoic ideal and a deprecation of God's creation. Any yielding to the needs of the body, especially in sex, was militantly to be stamped out.

St. John Climacus praises the monk who wrapped his hand in his cassock when about to carry his sick mother. And says to ''deaden your hand to natural or unnatural things, whether your own or another's body.''[5]

The dualism of Gnosticism had its influence also in the deprecation of the human body by certain monks. Many of their austere, bodily mortifications could be explained by the Gnostic axiom, ''My body kills me; therefore I kill it.''[6] Several heretical sects developed through a mingling of Gnostic and Christian principles. The *Encratites* (who abstained from marriage, meat, wine and so forth) won the admiration of many orthodox Christians by the intensity of their bodily feats of mortification. No doubt this explains the fervor of the Christian monks in the desert who felt an obligation to perform even more feats in the name of Christianity than those performed by heretics.

But in spite of some monks falling into an unchristian attitude toward the body and an unhealthy attitude toward withdrawal from the world that led to a dehumanizing of their personalities, still the majority of desert Fathers grew in true sanctity through a healthy spirituality that still contains important elements for those of us in the 20th century. Basically, when we read the writings of the monks of the desert, we react negatively to their flight from the world. It does seem that they accepted the Neoplatonic principle that the highest good a human person could attain in this life was knowledge of himself through concentration upon the interior movements of his spiritual powers and self-discipline lived out in as complete a solitude and silence as possible.

What true interpretation can we find in defense of their lives and in profit for our own spiritual lives today? The key to understanding their lives and writings lies in understanding as they did the tension between what lacked authenticity in their lives and in the "world" around them and what was possible in the striving for true authenticity with the help of God's divinizing grace. Fundamentally they teach us that human existence is a tensioned living, not between the physical body and the spirit, not between a choice to live in the world or in the desert away from other human beings, but between our basic "fallenness" by which we tend toward self-centeredness and not toward God-centeredness, and what can be possible by grace and his cooperation. All human beings, in all times and in all places, tend to become absorbed in immediate concerns that take us away from ultimate concern. We forget how we are bound into a slavery to our senses and live in a continual state of "forgetting" our true destiny as children of God. The Fathers call this state of being thrown into a whirling confusion and off-centeredness, "*mataia merimna*," a state of preoccupation with vain cares. Jesus had preached against such a preoccupation for the things one eats and puts on, an absorption that takes one away from seeking seriously and completely the kingdom of God (Lk 12:22-31).

St. Paul warns of the danger of being "tossed to and fro and carried about with every wind of doctrine by the cunning of

men'' (Eph 4:14; cf. Heb 13:9). The monks of the desert, in using the mythopoetic language and symbolism of Holy Scripture,
link up the world, the devil and the flesh to this whirling preoccupation with nonessential things to express what Heidegger
calls human inauthenticity. Such mythical language, so rooted
in scripture, as R. Bultmann has pointed out in his works on
demythologizing such biblical myths, is expressing a truth about
the human condition that is so real, so vast in its universal repercussions, that simple black-and-white concepts could never express it. Yet such mythical language, if it is to be effective in
relaying new knowledge, must be experienced in the depths of
one's psychical and spiritual life. An example of such language
by the two hesychastic Fathers, Callistus and Ignatius, is found
in their *Directions to Hesychasts:*

> The seduction and undying enmity towards us of the redoubt-
> able *Belial* teach us to turn away from the soul-saving command-
> ments of God, and to be tossed hither and thither in rapids
> which wreck the soul. [7]

That we might better understand just what the Fathers
were saying in the use of such mythopoetic language, let us look
at Heidegger's more modern attempt to describe basically the
same human condition that concerned the desert Fathers. According to Heidegger, *care* is made up of *facticity, possibility*
and *fallenness.*

In our *facticity,* we are defined by our being there (*Da-sein*)
in a particular place and time, ''thrown'' into a limited world
from which we cannot separate our existence.

In our *possibility,* however, we are opened to the future,
that which is never finished. But this *possibility* is still defined
by our *facticity.* The basic problem of all of us is the constant
tendency to ignore our *possibility* and to immerse ourselves
completely in the present. This state of *facticity* is precarious
when ignored and describes what biblically is meant by our
fallenness.

John Macquarrie builds upon Heidegger's concepts to see in the *world,* therefore, two aspects. It can be the place for our future development according to our potential; it can be seen as an inimical force threatening our true existence. He writes:

> The complete existential concept of the world has therefore two sides to it: (a)The world is an instrumental system, a workshop, to be understood in relation to man's practical concern; (b)The world is a threat to man's authentic existence, insofar as he can lose himself in it, and conceal from himself the difference between his own being and the being of what is within the world.[8]

Both the Old and the New Testament and the hesychastic writers maintain this distinction. In such writings we clearly see the world referred to as God's creation that he sees as good and that we must cooperate with so as to serve God's glory and provide for a share in our happiness. The spirituality of flight from the world stresses the danger in "practical concern," insofar as it may tend to immerse us in the day-to-day present and lead us to identify with the objects around us. This distinction between world as instrument to be used to serve God's glory and world as obstacle to the kingdom of God is clearly brought out in the following text written by St. Isaac of Syria in the seventh century:

> When you hear that it is necessary to withdraw from the world, to leave the world, to purify yourself from all that belongs to the world, you must first learn and understand the term *world,* not in its everyday meaning, but in its purely inward significance. When you understand what it means and the different things that this term includes, you will be able to learn about your soul—how far removed it is from the world and what is mixed with it that is of the world. "World" is a collective name, embracing what are called passions. When we want to speak of passions collectively, we call them "the world"; when we want to distinguish between them according to their different names, we call them passions.[9]

THE MEANINGS OF SILENCE AND SOLITUDE

If we keep in mind, therefore, this double meaning of "world," we can interpret the meanings of silence and solitude as found in the writings of the hesychastic Fathers and in nearly all other Christian mystics. The desert Fathers knew that Christianity was a divinizing process that took place gradually within the human "heart," the interior focus where man and the triune God meet. It is in the heart of man that God is constantly speaking his Word through his Spirit of love. The hesychastic Fathers were only being scriptural when they used the heart as the place where man encounters God both with his existential self that at times needs healing from God and with his transformed, gifted self as a "new creature" in Jesus Christ. Solitude is more than being alone and separated from other persons. Silence is more than not speaking.

Solitude is the withdrawal from the multiplicity of "worldly" cares to enter into a oneness with God. Such a withdrawal admits of many degrees. Arsenius, one of the early monks who left the Byzantine court to flee into the desert, had heard a voice telling him to *"fuge, tace et quiesce,"* "flee, keep silent and be at rest." These three injunctions are more or less at the core of the hesychastic spirituality. They demand a fleeing, a withdrawal from the spirit of the world and a silence, at least an interior silence of the heart. The *quies (hesychia* in Greek) is the necessary tranquillity wherein the total being becomes integrated, so that there is no more self-seeking dispersion of the passions in all directions. Everything is coordinated and under the influence of grace.

Both silence and solitude, therefore, must be interpreted in hesychastic language in symbolic form to embrace various levels of attentive listening to God's Word as it is being spoken within the individual and in the events of everyday life. Besides the evident physical withdrawal and maximum "aloneness" that the hesychasts continually prized and eagerly sought after, they taught a silence and solitude that highlighted a movement inwardly toward a more spiritual listening to God's indwelling presence. This second stage of withdrawal, as Archimandrite Kallistos Ware describes,[10] is the spirituality of aloneness and silence in the monk's cell. This is a "localization" in a physical sense within a community of monks or even lay persons living in the world wherein one turns into a quiet place and cuts off further communications with others in order to stand in a state of alertness and remembrance of God's presence.

The true silence and solitude that are necessary for not only monks but for all Christians, regardless of their style of life, are summarized in the phrase, "return into oneself." This is a state of soul where the real desert is found in the heart. St. Basil describes such a return to oneself:

> When the mind is no longer dissipated amidst external things nor dispersed across the world through the senses, it returns to itself; and by means of itself it ascends to the thought of God.[11]

This is the stage of silence and solitude that brings about a true inner stillness and a state of attentive listening and total surrender to God's Word heard in the depths of one's being.

Such inner silence and solitude, aloneness with God, lead to the spiritual poverty that Jesus blessed and equated with the kingdom of heaven (Mt 5:3; Lk 6:20). It is the kenotic state of self-emptying so that our activity of speaking and controlling God by words and images yields to an active receptivity that is the sign of love lived out in self-surrender and mystery. It is "praying in the heart" that is a gift of the Holy Spirit who prays within us without our words but with God's single, unspoken Word (Rom 8:26-27). St. Gregory of Sinai describes this emptying of the mind of all thoughts to be alone with God:

> But it is not good for those who practice silence, for whom it is more fitting to abide in God alone, praying in their heart and refraining from thought. For, according to John of the Ladder [Climacus] silence means setting aside thoughts about things, whether of the senses or the mind. . . . For our God is peace, being above all speech and tumult.[12]

APPLICATIONS

Much that we find written, not only in the works of the hesychastic Fathers, but in the writings of Western mystics, speaks of flight from the world and living in silence and solitude. The authors were usually celibate monks or nuns who led a life that allowed for a literal flight from the multifaceted world of commerce; of men, women and children living in cities, of daily work in a technological setting; in general, a world that is truly at all sides "groaning in travail" (Rom 8:19-23). Reading such works we might turn away in disgust as we falsely interpret their motives for such withdrawal and also as we see the impossibility of our own achieving of such a state before we can ever get on with deeper prayer. We might even have an advanced sense of true incarnationalism that shows us the possibility of meeting Jesus Christ in technology and precisely inside of the "world" and be even less receptive to the message of such writers. Or we might think that such a literal withdrawal is absolutely necessary and thus seek to run from our responsible commitments to those living in the "world."

But in presenting an interpretation of this language that sees it on many levels of being, we can see that there is much for us to learn in the teaching of such spiritual giants of earlier days. Regardless of whether we live very much "in the world" or are relatively withdrawn from immediate contact with the multiplicity of the world, we are called to flee away from the vain cares of the "world, the flesh and the devil" and enter into an interior desert. The more we put off the flight into that desert, the more we will tend, whether we live either in the physical desert or in the world, to be "carnal-minded" or unspiritual like the Christians who have not surrendered interiorly to the inner guidance of the Holy Spirit (Rom 8:3-11).

Thomas Merton describes the true meaning of withdrawal that should apply to all of us, and not merely monks:

> This is the secret of monastic "renunciation of the world." Not a denunciation, not a denigration, not a precipitous flight, a

resentful withdrawal, but a liberation, a kind of permanent "vacation" in the original sense of "emptying." The monk simply discards the useless and tedious baggage of vain concerns and devotes himself henceforth to the one thing really necessary—the one thing that he really wants: the quest for meaning and for love, the quest for his own identity, his secret name promised him by God (Rv 2:17) and for the peace of Christ which the world cannot give (Jn 14:27).[13]

If we are desirous of experiencing God, we must resolutely journey inwardly, away from the worldly and vain cares that keep us centered exclusively upon ourselves, our "false self." Our true self lies deep within us, as a seed hidden in the earth. By returning to our "heart" we find our deepest center by consciously opening up to the loving presence of the triune God dwelling within us. Without such an "aloneness" within our heart we will never know our true identity which has from all eternity been linked together in the mind of the heavenly Father with his Logos-made-flesh, Jesus Christ. Our search for true authenticity can never be found in the illusory world that does not recognize God as the beginning and end of all creation and of all life.

The more we are diffused and distracted by objects outside ourselves, the less conscious is our prayer and the less unifying is our union of mind with the mind of God in a loving surrender. We fear to let go of our controlled levels of existence. Yet God calls us into a silence and solitude of the heart where all artificiality crumbles, and new psychic and spiritual powers burgeon forth, released through the uncreated energies of God. God silently whispers, "Be still, and know that I am God" (Ps 46:10).[14] Silence on these psychic and spiritual levels is the interior air that the spirit needs in order to grow. Such silence leads into the inner recess of our being and there our heavenly Father will recompense us (Mt 6:6). This recompensing comes in the healing of psychic disturbances, the chaotic meaninglessness of so many past experiences that hang like dried skeletons within the memory, the anxieties that force us into an isolation of deadly loneliness. We become consoled and loved by God in an experience that is beyond concepts. We know that we know God loves us. This being-loved-by-God experience at the deepest level of our consciousness restores our strength and pushes us to new self-giving and creativity.

SILENCE

One of the greatest needs we have in our modern living is the need for silence. Noise permeates our lives. Even when we retire in the evening to sleep, noises of city life surround us. We become tense and our nights are filled with restless tossing and disturbing dreams. We are being pulled in so many directions. Our lives rush by with such rapidity that we could wake up only to discover that we are at the end of our life and we have not even begun to live. Thus we need to leave our fragmented, noisy world and enter into the primeval, endless *now* of God's eternal silence. This is not a cowardly retreat. This is where life and love merge into the same experience.

And yet what courage it takes to break away from the "herd" and find time to be silent and alone with God: We cannot search for authenticity except in withdrawing from our world of illusions. Yet we protect the images and masks that conceal from us our true face. The problem today is the problem of the solitary. We need to build a deeper self and become the "new man" (our true self) being liberated from the "old man" (our false self). This is the first lesson that we can draw from the desert spirituality. The desert monks were fundamentally Christians in honest search for their true selves in Christ. To reach this level of truth they had to shed the false self fabricated under social compulsion in the world of their times. They sought a way through the darkness of the heart, guided only by the Holy Spirit. They tore up the maps furnished them by those who lived in the "world," the world of illusion that offers the self, not God, as the center of life.

But uprooting the familiar is similar to the Israelites leaving the fleshpots of Egypt only to enter into the dark, still, foreboding desert of Sinai. In such vast nothingness there is only God and the hope of our true self coming to birth in such stilling of our own noisy activities. Merton describes the anguish of such a step into silence:

> The man who wants to deepen his existential awareness has to make a break with ordinary existence and this break is costly. It cannot be made without anguish and suffering. It implies loneliness and the disorientation of one who has to recognize that the old signposts don't show him the way and that in fact he has to find the way by himself without a map.[15]

If we wish to grow in true prayer and pray always, to become listeners of God's Word, we must learn to carve out some segment of our busy days for silence and solitude. There are some times during the year when we can truly withdraw from the ''world'' by touching the silence of God and entering into the silence of nature. Yet even in such physical silence our hearts can still be very busy about many things. Just as the hermits of the desert cut themselves off from the busy world, so too we must take the first step toward inner silence and aloneness with God by finding moments of entering into physical silence. Even the busiest person will find such moments if he or she sincerely seeks them. Once we are convinced of the necessity of such moments of quiet for deeper communion with God, we will find time in our busy day for such withdrawal.

These moments will be found in early morning or during the night in breaking our sleep to rise and adore God in ''silence and in truth.'' Our hearts will thirst as the doe thirsts for living waters (Ps 42) and we will find shorter moments, like a sigh or a gasp, to turn within and surrender our lives to God during the active part of the day. Before retiring in the evening, we will enter into the desert of the heart and silence the noisiness and clamoring of our being in order to enter into the seventh day of resting with the healing love of God.

Without such quiet moments there can be no growth in

deeper, prayerful union with God. Attentive listening to the Word of God is a dying process to that autonomous, "managerial" hold that we have on our own life, on the lives of others and, above all, on God as we either forget him in our busyness or fashion images of him that become static little idols before which we bow and do reverence. But the living God of Abraham, Isaac and Jacob waits for us in the desert of our silent selves to reveal himself to us in his own time and in his own words.

Many persons serious about deeper prayer have turned away from the outside, distracting noises only to find more deafening noises inside their minds. Great discipline of the mind is needed to uproot such noise and find that inner peace and tranquillity that can come only if the mind is focused more deeply upon God as the inner fortress of our strength. This requires a constant state of *conversion,* a *metanoia* or turning totally to God as the center of all our values. This conversion consists of a greater and greater surrender to the creative action of the indwelling Trinity in our heart. Such a conversion can be measured only by the change we experience in perceptions and values in our life.

Bernard Lonergan describes conversion as taking place on four different levels of human consciousness. We can consider each level a degree of entering into greater psychical or spiritual silence and solitude, an aloneness with the Alone. He calls them the empirical, intellectual, rational and responsible levels.[16] As we move in the lower levels of conversion away from our habitual ways of sensing, perceiving, feeling, speaking and moving and from our manner of understanding and expressing what we have understood, we move to the rational level of reflecting and passing judgment on what we have reflected. This leads to the responsible level where we evaluate, decide and carry out our decisions.[17]

It is on this responsible level that we reach true silence and solitude that is a gift of God, attained through a childlike trust, joy and peace in the embrace of the indwelling Trinity. Such a silence flows from the deep union with God, moving outwardly to effect, not only a deeper silence of the mind, but a silence that affects also the very way that we look at others, the way we smile, the way we walk and talk. In such a deep experience of God's direct and immediate love, Father, Son and Holy Spirit, we enter into a sharing of the freedom of Jesus who took responsibility over his life by seeking at every moment, especially in his agony and death, to turn his whole being over to his heavenly Father in meaningful, self-surrendering love. When we enter into such silencing of our own plans and desires for our lives and place our lives totally under the dominion of God's good pleasure, we enter into the true responsibility that is the maturity of the children of God. It is a total and permanent self-surrender without conditions, qualifications or reservations. It is a "being-in-love in an unrestricted fashion."[18]

SPIRITUAL POVERTY

As we enter more deeply into our true self, we move away from the noises and multifaceted world that our false self has been continually absorbed in, thus preventing our genuine listening to God's Word. We enter into a silence that becomes truly a spiritual poverty, the result of experiencing the infinite riches of God's love for us as the Father begets within our heart the very presence of Jesus. We begin to enter into the strange paradox that Jesus spoke of, of losing our life in order to find it. As the Holy Spirit lets his light of truth shine upon our true self, we become not only filled with a sense of our nothingness and sinfulness before the beauty of the All-Holy, but we become broken in spirit. No longer is there the independent Eve-element in us that wants to be like God. Our self-assurance dissolves as the Spirit begins to unfold to us our true identity as children of God being loved into being by the interacting love of a Father begetting his Son in his Spirit.

We stand emptied before the richness of God. What can we say? God's love is spoken in silence and in our emptying silence we hear his Word as Love experienced. "My sacrifice is this broken spirit. You will not scorn this crushed and broken heart" (Ps 51:17). Inner poverty and silence coalesce before the awesome presence of the Lord that is revealed in his immanent tenderness to only the "little ones." True inner silence becomes loving surrender as we no longer have any words to say to God. God must reveal himself in his Word and we can only wait for him to speak his one Word in silence. "Speak, Yahweh, your servant is listening" (1 Sm 3:9).

This paradox of emptying ourselves in order to become filled with the "utter fullness of God" (Eph 3:19) has been aptly described by Thomas Merton:

> All the paradoxes about the contemplative way are reduced to this one: being without desire means being led by a desire so great that it is incomprehensible. . . . It is a blind desire, which seems like a desire for "nothing" only because nothing can content it. . . . But true emptiness is that which transcends all things, and yet is immanent in all. For what seems to be emptiness in this case is pure being. It is not this, not that. . . . The character of emptiness, at least for a Christian contemplative, is pure love, pure freedom. Love that is free of everything, not determined by any thing or held down by any special relationship. It is love for love's sake. It is a sharing, through the Holy Spirit, in the infinite charity of God. . . . This purity, freedom and indeterminateness of love is the very essence of Christianity.[19]

Such inner silence is a relinquishing of all thoughts and images about God. It is an entering into a state of true knowledge of self and of God that is sheer gift of the Holy Spirit. This state is called "purity of heart" by Cassian and the other early Fathers and called "humility" in the total history of Christian spiritual writers. Evagrius writes of this inner stillness from all cares and all thoughts: "You will not be able to pray purely if you are all involved with material affairs and agitated with unremitting concerns. For prayer is the rejection of concepts."[20]

The hesychastic Fathers give us the first great lesson if we are to pray incessantly in our hearts. They knew that all Christians could not literally leave the multiplied "world," as the Fathers themselves were singularly inspired to do. But this one thing they were sure of: All Christians who wish to listen to God's Word speak to them of his infinite love for them individually must go into their hearts and there live in the silence of complete detachment from self and the created world of persons and things. God is silent within himself. The Begetter and the Begotten and the unifying Love between them are relationships of loving presence that unfold in silence, in ultimate humility and self-sacrificing love for the Other.

Only we, of all God's creatures, are able to "listen" to God's silent love by faith within our hearts. We alone are temples of God being constantly begotten children of God by the uncreated energies of the loving, triune God within us. St. Ignatius of Antioch grasped the relationship between the silence of God and the necessity of Christians to listen in silence to God as he speaks his Word within them:

> Anyone who is really possessed of the word of Jesus can listen to his silence and so be perfect; so that he may act through his words and be known by his silence.[21]

Inner attentiveness to the Word of God that is constantly speaking from within our hearts about the Father's infinite love for us is an obligation for all Christians, regardless of lifestyle. The desert Fathers teach us this absolute necessity of inner silence, of reaching the state of *hesychia* or resting in active self-surrender to God's loving presence. Nicholas Cabasilas of the 14th century, who worked as a layman in the court of Constantinople and yet strove to live the ideal of other hesychasts who lived in monasteries or in the desert, writes to us in the modern world:

> And everyone should keep his art or profession. The general should continue to command; the farmer to till the land; the ar-

tisan to practice his craft. And I will tell you why. It is not necessary to retire into the desert, to take unpalatable food, to alter one's dress, to compromise one's health, or to do anything unwise, because it is quite possible to remain in one's own home without giving up all one's possessions, and yet to practice continual meditation.[22]

There is no style of life, no work, no place, no person that can prevent us from reaching this inward state of interior silence that leads to true poverty of spirit. Such poverty of spirit is described by Jesus as the kingdom of God living within us. All Christians are to seek the kingdom of God with all their hearts (Mt 6:33) and to forget all else as ends outside of their existing value in God. We are to seek God with our whole heart, strength and mind. This seeking of God as the prime focus of our lives is true single-heartedness. It is our integration into the unique person that God knows us to be in his eternal love.

For a person who has begun the inner journey into the heart, true prayer should no longer be a thing to do, an activity before God. It should become more and more a state of standing before God's loving presence, totally emptied of self, total gift to God. In complete nudity of spirit, in complete formlessness, without words, but with the "passionless passion" of the total true self, we grow daily in oneness with the triune God. We learn that all the light from our own intellectual powers is but a darkness that yields to a new light of God's self-revelation through his Word that is heard in utter silence. Prayer of the heart becomes the unremitting consciousness of God's abiding presence deep within us. It brings about the state of restfulness, tranquillity, the quelling of all inordinate movements and desires, passions and thoughts within us.

In such integration we find ourselves in a new oneness with all other human beings. The closer we touch God as the supreme center of our lives, the closer we touch all other human beings who are constantly being drawn to that eternal Center by God's uncreated energies of love.

Evagrius defines a true Christian in terms of a good monk: "A monk is a man who considers himself one with all men because he seems constantly to see himself in every man."[23] Our inner poverty fills us with joy in experiencing the great richness of the Father who begets all his children and bestows upon them a universe of manifold beauty and riches. "In him we live and move and have our being" (Acts 17:28). The Holy Spirit makes us realize that, at the heart of matter and of the whole created world, including ourselves and all other persons that we meet, the Trinity lives a mystery of love, the love of three Persons in their reciprocal relationship to one another. As we experience this basic reality of loving communion that exists among the divine Persons in self-surrender through their Spirit of Love, we can go forth into our daily, busy lives and pray always. Then it is no longer in spite of the world and our work in the world that we must find time to pray, but it is precisely in our present world and through our daily "busyness" in our work that we move from the poverty of our spirit to touch the richness of God's Spirit, working out of love in all events.

We move outward to create a similar community of self-sacrificing persons. We contemplate God everywhere with new eyes. We see this world undergoing a gradual transfiguration by the inner life of God and we are called to be reconcilers of the whole world through Christ to the Father (2 Cor 5:19). The great message of the desert athletes, who emptied themselves so dramatically on the physical, psychical and spiritual levels, is this: To the degree that we have purified and disciplined ourselves to sit before the Lord and to listen to his Word, to that extent we can stand before the world and witness to the Word in loving service. God really does fill the empty with good things. Withdrawal paradoxically means finding God everywhere and returning to all men to serve them in self-sacrificing love. Silence is paradoxically a listening, and solitude is truly finding the whole world in God.

3.

PRAYING IN THE HEART

As human beings, we have been made, not only for communication, but for communion, a sharing of one another through love. Our words are symbols chosen to express an inner meaningfulness, a desire for more of an already existing actuality of love. Our whole life, with all that we do and say and act out and react to, is a symbol expressing this inner urge for communion with an other or others through love.

Boris Pasternak, the widely known Soviet writer, expresses this in the words that he places in the mouth of Nikolai Nikolaievich in *Doctor Zhivago:*

> Let me tell you what I think. I think that if the beast who sleeps in man could be held down by threats—any kind of threats, whether of jail or of retribution after death (by some transcendent God)—then the highest emblem of humanity would be the lion tamer in the circus with his whip, not the prophet who sacrificed himself. But don't you see, this is just the point—what has for centuries raised man above the beast is not the cudgel but an inward music: the irresistible power of unarmed truth, the powerful attraction of its example. It has always been assumed that the most important things in the Gospels are the ethical maxims and commandments. But for me the most important thing is that Christ speaks in parables taken from life; that he explains the truth in terms of everyday reality. The idea that underlines this is that communion between mortals is immortal, and that the whole of life is symbolic because it is meaningful.[1]

It is in human love relations that we discover the loving beauty of God. This beauty we call transcendent, because it can never be captured, possessed, held within us in a static complacency. We yearn to be set on fire by the ever-new levels of union with God that we can, by God's condescending love and mercy, attain. As we experience a sense of identity in the union of love through an expanded state of consciousness, we always want more of the same awareness. We cannot live without it. And yet attaining new growth in love with a human person or God brings an awful pain. There is so much more to possess! There is also an agonizing look into our nothingness and the self-centeredness that we know must be put to death if we are to reach new levels of love. And we do not like the thought of death!

INCESSANT PRAYER

The Fathers of the desert were strongly seized by the love of God. It burned in their hearts and drove them into the desert to attain ever-increasing levels of loving union with God. They did not believe that the injunctions found in Holy Scripture were mere hyperbole or that their fulfillment was for a select group of elite Christians using certain techniques or living a particular style of life. They felt that Jesus exhorts *all* Christians to pray continually. "Then Jesus told them a parable about the need to pray continually and never lose heart" (Lk 18:1). Jesus had said "Watch you, therefore, and pray always. . ." (Lk 21:36).[2] St. Paul clearly encouraged the early Christians never to cease praying:

> Be happy at all times; pray constantly; and for all things give thanks to God, because this is what God expects you to do in Christ Jesus (1 Thes 5:17-18).

The Fathers of the desert sought to enter into their "heart" and there, with God's grace, push themselves to a constant remembrance of God's loving presence. They realized that prayer was more than saying prayers, asking God for gifts and even giving thanks for gifts received. It was a *state* of being, of living beyond the habitual idea that they had of themselves or that their society fashioned for them. It was a continued journey within, a return to their true selves, by living as consciously as possible in loving surrender to God as their Source and their End.

Is such incessant prayer, or what they called "prayer of the heart" or "pure prayer," possible for human beings? The best of the desert Fathers felt that it was, with God's grace. They felt that this was the goal of the Christian life: to surrender completely at all times in love to please the heavenly Father. The means was to strive to obtain purity of heart through desire and ascetical practices aimed at uprooting self-centered love and developing the Christ-like virtues.

No matter how austere their practices of asceticism in order to reach purity of heart, they knew that only the Holy Spirit could gift them with such a state of constant prayer. It is the Spirit who pours out into emptied hearts the gifts of faith, hope and love to uproot any false images about God and about oneself; who enables a person to surrender all anxieties in child-like trust in the heavenly Father and to live in constant love toward God and neighbor, the sign of how *divinized* an individual Christian has become. Such a person has new, interior eyes, those of the spirit, that allow him or her to live in God's truth, according to an "inward music."

> These are the very things that God has revealed to us through the Spirit, for the Spirit reaches the depths of everything, even the depths of God. After all, the depths of a man can only be known by his own spirit, not by any other man, and in the same way the depths of God can only be known by the Spirit of God. Now instead of the spirit of the world, we have received the Spirit that comes from God, to teach us to understand the gifts that he has given us. . . . A spiritual man, on the other hand, is able to judge the value of everything, and his own value is not to be judged by other men. . . . But we are those who have the mind of Christ (1 Cor 2:10-16).

HOW TO PRAY ALWAYS

Convinced that all Christians were called to pray incessantly, the Fathers strove to fulfill this injunction from the New Testament. But how can one pray always since "pray" means to say prayers either vocally or silently, and "always" implies doing nothing but praying? Even the monks of the desert realized that they had to work for a living; they needed to eat and sleep. One group of early Christians who fell into an exaggerated literalism of this injunction, the *Messalians* (Syriac: *Mesaliane* meaning "the ones who pray"), felt that any kind of work or occupation incompatible with actual exterior prayer was to be condemned.[3] Various other more sane and orthodox Fathers recognized the impossibility of such a belief and sought to bring the Messalians to their senses by refusing to support them with food when they refused to work.

The majority of the Fathers realized that true, incessant prayer did not mean literally saying explicit prayers continually. Origen taught that good works and the observance of the commandments do not interrupt true prayer. For him, to pray without ceasing is to unite prayer to necessary works. Prayer, for Origen, is a raising of the mind toward God. A person's "prayerfulness" is determined by the degree to which his actions and prayerful attitude arise from the love of God.[4]

St. Augustine built upon Origen's teaching to show that incessant prayer is possible for all Christians if they direct all of their actions toward the good pleasure of God. "Hence it is in faith, hope and charity that we pray with a perpetual desire of doing so."[5] But the further question that the Fathers asked and sought to live out was: If all actions are to be done out of love for God, how can we think always of God?

Evagrius, the philosopher and spiritual teacher of desert contemplation in the fourth century, sees spiritual contemplation as a state of "pure intellectuality." Such pure prayer, as Evagrius described it, was the state in which all mental concepts, thoughts, images, all multiplicity, all reasoning had been excluded. From the negative side, the withdrawal from all multiplicity, the source of all inordinate passions, would bring the monk to *apatheia,* the state of passionlessness. This, for Evagrius, is not apathy but a "passionate passionlessness" which defines charity as the superior state of reasonable love in which it is impossible to love what would be in this world more than the knowledge of God.

But such a description and such a reality hardly seem within the grasp of every person, and the New Testament teaching is for all. The majority of the desert Fathers saw prayer, not in terms of the strong intellectual accent that Evagrius gave to the subject, but rather in terms of the *praxis* or ascetical life along with the inner "pushing" of one's consciousness always more toward God as the goal of all one's actions or thoughts. The school of Macarius and of the writers of Mount Sinai, such as John Climacus, Hesychius, Philotheus and Nil, describe incessant prayer as a "straining toward God." While giving themselves to manual labor and the other duties of their life such monks invented special mental formulas or ejaculations that were repeated as often as the monks could call them to mind.

This is the beginning of the Jesus Prayer that centers around a phrase, including the name of Jesus, repeated as often as the person can do so, accompanied by an interior desire to be in the presence of the Lord and Savior. The prayer element consists in the longing and the stretching out spiritually toward the Lord. Usually such a formula contains an element stressing compunction and the "sinful" condition of man. For the monks of the desert who cried out as often as they could from the depths of their hearts, God was experienced as a God of love and infinite richness. At the same time they experienced their own essential poverty and inability to extricate themselves from their "fallen" state of inauthenticity.

REMEMBRANCE OF GOD

Not contradicting the above-mentioned elements of the

prayer of the heart, St. Basil and many others who followed his prudent doctrine on praying always give us an added dimension that brings such constant prayer into the orbit of the ordinary person living in the world. St. Basil realized that the ordinary Christian could not give himself or herself continually to the recitation, orally or mentally, of a fixed ejaculation as a way of centering upon God. He coined the phrase, "attend to yourself," to refer to an inner attentiveness or a state of alert consciousness of God's ever-abiding presence and an active desire on the part of the individual to bring himself or herself into harmony with God's holy will manifested at every moment. St. Basil well understood the dignity to which we human beings have been called by God. We do not merely remember that God is the goal of our lives, but we are also able to direct and guide our actions toward God. St. Basil describes such attentiveness as the basis for incessant prayer:

> We should watch over our heart with all vigilance not only to avoid ever losing the thought of God or sullying the memory of his wonders by vain imaginations, but also in order to carry about the holy thoughts of God stamped upon our souls as an ineffaceable seal by continuous and pure recollection . . . so the Christian directs every action, small and great, according to the will of God, performing the action at the same time with care and exactitude, and keeping his thoughts fixed upon the One who gave him the work to do. In this way he fulfills the saying, "I set the Lord always in my sight; for he is at my right hand, that I be not moved" and he also observes the precept, "Whether you eat or drink or whatsoever else you do, do all to the glory of God.". . .We should perform every action as if under the eyes of the Lord and think every thought as if observed by him . . . fulfilling the words of the Lord: "I seek not my own will but the will of him that sent me, the Father."[6]

Incessant prayer in Basil's doctrine moves away from (but does not disfavor) the constant thinking about God or the recitation of an ejaculation and centers on the ability of an individual to direct his or her will to want to remain in the continued remembrance of God's presence. If a person does not have this desire to remember God's loving presence, then even the constant recitation of prayers and the performance of good works will not be pleasing to God. It is such remembrance of God that allows the Christian to direct all of his or her thoughts, words and actions toward God. God is the beginning and end of such a Christian's life, realized in the concrete moment of living.

INTERPRETATION

We who live in the 20th century can easily dismiss the efforts of the early Christians to pray always by seeking to push themselves at each moment to higher levels of awareness of God's loving presence. Such Christians surely lived in a more simplified society with less noise and anxieties than we find in our urban life today. But what are the important elements to us in their teaching about praying in the heart? How can we sift through the elements that are not so applicable to the ordinary Christian's life today and come up with the perennial, true doctrine that should be lived by all of us if we wish to call ourselves dynamic Christians?

If God is love, he is always actively giving himself to total self-emptying to us. True prayer, without which one cannot be a true Christian, must be a state of ever-increasing transformation into the activity of God that is love. This is the essential doctrine of the New Testament, the purpose of the Incarnation and Redemption, namely, that we human beings have been chosen by God's gratuitous selection to share in his very own trinitarian life. We are called to become divinized through the Holy Spirit who effects within us a regeneration. This is the teaching of the early Fathers on *theosis* or divinization of man through God's grace, making him a true participator in God's very own nature (2 Pt 1:4). This is not an extrinsic, moral resemblance to God but a conscious relationship in loving union in which we become our true selves to the degree that we live in the oneness of the Father, Son and Holy Spirit.

Prayer of the heart is ultimately the operation of the indwelling Trinity living within us. By God's loving activities we become one in heart with the trinitarian community. Cassian, who traveled for many years among the desert Fathers and lived with them, brought their teachings to the West. He established in Marseilles a monastery for men and another for women and wrote his *Conferences* and his *Institutes*. He expresses this loving activity of God within the Christian:

> For then will be perfectly fulfilled in our case the prayer of our Savior in which he prayed for his disciples to the Father saying: "that the love wherewith thou lovedst me may be in them and they in us," and again: "that they may all be one in us" (Jn 17:21,26), that they may be one as thou, Father, in me and I in thee, that they may be one in us when that perfect love of God, wherewith "He first loved us" (1 Jn 4:19) has passed into the feelings of our heart as well, by the fulfillment of this prayer of the Lord which we believe cannot possibly be ineffectual.[7]

Prayer of the heart is not a technique or even a certain stage in the total process of growth in prayer. The hesychastic Fathers constantly describe it as forcing the mind down into the heart. It is basically an affective attitude that seeks to transcend the limitations of human words and mental images to reach an inner "still point" where God and man meet in silent self-surrender.

St. Theophan, the Russian recluse, describes this attitude:

> Prayer is turning the mind and thoughts towards God. To pray means to stand before God with the mind, mentally to gaze unswervingly at him, to converse with him in reverent fear and hope. . . . The principal thing is to stand with the mind in the heart before God and to go on standing before him unceasingly day and night, until the end of life. . . . Behave as you wish, so long as you learn to stand before God with the mind in the heart, for in this lies the essence of the matter.[8]

In such deep, interior prayer, we hunger to possess more consciously the living presence of the Risen Lord Jesus. We seek a "circumcision of the heart," such as the Prophet Jeremiah preached to the Israelites, "Circumcise yourselves for Yahweh; off with the foreskin of your hearts" (Jer 4:4). It is into the "heart," our deepest level of consciousness of ourselves as free and loving persons, that we must go in order to experience intimately and profoundly God's great love for us. It is in the heart that we find the "inner closet" that Jesus spoke of (Mt 6:6) and where we adore our Father in silence and in truth.

It is there also that we, in courage and in humility, look at the dark shadows of our nature. We encounter face to face the demonic forces from all of our past experiences that lie repressed under the masks, fancy speeches and spiritual poses that we formerly considered essential to our prayer.

PURITY OF HEART

Jesus promised that those who were pure of heart would see God (Mt 5:8). The hesychastic Fathers speak about the prayer of the heart as synonymous with the attainment of purity of heart. Yet they never describe either of these in detail. They exhort Christians to seek both as though they were the same thing. Techniques and teachings on acquiring virtues and on extirpating any inordinate desires are amply given in their writings. But they knew that no one could adequately describe prayer and purity of heart to someone who had not yet experienced them. And for those who had begun the journey inward and made the surrender to the indwelling Trinity, a description was not necessary.

Prayer of the heart is a "knowing" as used in the biblical sense. To "know" meant to know something or someone experientially, as a man "knew" his wife through their marriage relationship. This was never a cerebral knowledge only but a "real" knowing in the "heart." This was a "seeing" because the heart was pure. We can better understand the hesychastic meaning of purity by taking the example of light seen directly and through a glass. In the first case we can say that we see through the light. We cannot touch that through which we are seeing. But in seeing light through a glass we look through the glass, which can be touched, and it is the medium through which we see the light. It is in the ephemeral experience of light rather than in the more substantial experience of a tangible glass that we are able to grasp what the Fathers mean in using the phrase "purity of heart."

Praying in the heart with purity of heart means an inner discipline of spiritual alertness that enables us to uproot all that leads to self-centeredness. It means also an inner intention to bring every thought, word and deed under the dominion of Jesus Christ for the glory of God (2 Cor 10:5; 1 Cor 10:31). But it means much more in the direct experience of prayer. It is a purity that is freed from images, from intermediaries, from sensible things. It implies a prayer of directness and immediacy, seeing light directly and not through the medium of a glass. God is spirit, perfect spirit. Thus in order to encounter him immediately, spirit-to-spirit, we must be immensely pure. We must be stripped of all that stands in the way of that encounter, even our images of him.

This does not mean that the Fathers saw no place for the world of the sensible, the intellect and images in the realm of prayer. But these touch the prayer that precedes and prepares for the more contemplative prayer that they called the prayer of the heart or pure prayer. God is seen as perfectly pure and perfectly spiritual in the prayer of the heart. The "impure" mind is a slave to images, symbols and concepts, since faith, hope and love have not been purified and highly developed through the infusion of the Holy Spirit. It can only approach God by means of the sensible. God has not rejected this way of coming to knowledge of things, but rather he works through the sensible, always, however, with the intention of bringing such a person to that level where he or she can communicate with God unaided by the sensible.

St. Isaac of Syria describes this dying to the sensible in order to enter into the heart by using the model used by St. Paul of the "outer" and the "inner" man:

> Until the outer man dies to the whole world, not only to sin, but also to every activity, and equally until the inner man dies to evil thoughts and the natural stirrings of the body weaken, so that sinful sweetness no longer arises in the heart, until then the sweetness of the Divine Spirit will not arise in a man, his members will not acquire purity in this life, Divine thoughts will not enter his soul, and will remain not sensed and not seen. And until in his heart a man has made passive the cares of life, except for the indispensable needs of his nature, and entrusts this care to God, spiritual ecstasy will not spring forth in him.[9]

Christian growth into the life in God is the movement of one's whole being into the Being of God, so that the one, whose spiritual life is described as praying in the heart, can legitimately think that he is "breathing" with God, or sharing God's breath. Pure prayer is spirit-to-spirit communication. It is the ability to converse with God in his language of silence, to share with him in his Being. The lover is not detained by created realities, but runs to the very heart, the center, the Spirit of the Beloved.

Cassian speaks the language of the hesychasts in describing such "fiery prayer":

> We are affected from the very bottom of the heart, so that we get at its meaning (of Holy Scripture) not by reading the text but by experience anticipating it. And so our mind will reach that incorruptible prayer. . . distinguished by the use of no words or utterances; but with the purpose of the mind all on fire, . . . produced through ecstasy of heart by some unaccountable keenness of spirit, and the mind being thus affected without the aid of the sense or any visible material pours it forth to God with groanings and sighs that cannot be uttered.[10]

PRAYER IS LOVE

Ultimately such prayer of the heart is the work of the Spirit coming to us in our weakness when we do not know how to pray as we ought (Rom 8:26-27). The Spirit fills us with the love of God to the degree that we have emptied our "hearts." No longer do we serve God out of fear or remuneration as a slave or a hireling but now we love the Father purely out of the joy of love itself. It is a free love given for no other reason than for itself.

The message of the desert Fathers to us about prayer is one of exhorting us to live constantly motivated by the pure love of God for himself. In such humble adoration, freed from all earthly attachments, we are able to return the whole world back to God out of love for him. Perfection, the goal of the Christian life, is attained only by love. All the ascetical practices, handed down to us by these desert Fathers, have meaning only insofar as they are aids to bring about true love of God in our hearts. The prayer of the heart as an unceasing state of prayer is possible only in the light of the Spirit who at every moment pours into our hearts greater love of God. As this love unites us with God, it fills us also with a similar, unselfish love for the entire world.

APPLICATIONS

Modern man is poverty-stricken when it comes to an appreciation of true love. All around us we see a false type of love that is a mockery of true love. Our lives are flooded with slogans of "Make love, not war." Modern psychology has given us the phrase, "a meaningful relationship," but so many interpret it to mean what gratifies the individual's sense of pleasure without any responsible commitment to the other person.

The Fathers left the world and retired into the desert to enter into the invisible warfare within their hearts. There they struggled day and night to put to death the demonic influences that prevented the presence of God from being experienced as perfect Love. Few of us will feel the call to withdraw into the physical desert. But all of us, by our baptism, should feel the call to be driven by the Spirit into the inner desert. We do have a physical desert all around us. It is not miles and miles of arid sand with no sign of verdant life. It is miles and miles of dirt and filth, noise and multiplicity that lead to nowhere. Pollution and pornography, suicide and violence are all around us in our cities. "On subway walls and tenement halls" we are to discover in the ordinary things of urban life the presence of a loving God calling us inwardly into our hearts.

God is everywhere, all around us, and this does not exclude our cities. The modern, urban pilgrim knows that he is always taking a risk, that he must be ready to be uprooted as he searches for the "absent God" who becomes present when he is ready to lose today's hold on his presence. We are challenged as never before not to close ourselves off from God's amazing revelation of himself in the most "ungodly" situations. But it is into our hearts that we must go to discover God's loving presence and transforming power. It is there that we are to experience the absence and the darkness, the holding and communion and the losing and searching that allow us to grow continually into a greater awareness of God's presence as love. In that love we become one with him and are empowered to bring the same unifying love to others who are separated from us and from their center, God.

There are many levels of application of the hesychastic prayer of the heart to modern life. The first benefit that we can receive from such a desert spirituality is that we, like those Fathers, desire to pray constantly. They point out in the vast desert that the basic, necessary meaning of our human existence is not to say prayers, but to move daily into greater awareness of God's intimate and immediate loving presence which is to be discovered or unveiled in each moment. They strove day and night to pray always by seeking as much as possible to do all for love of God.

We have been taught a spirituality also of seeking to do God's will at all times. But prayer-of-the-heart spirituality, coming out of the Old and New Testaments, is based on a process of continued experiencing God as uncreated energies of love, very near to us, actively drawing us into a share of his love. In our Western spirituality we were taught all too often to "say" prayers *to* God. He remained outside of us and we approached him in words and images. More serious Christians made "acts" of the presence of God. But his presence was as real as the actual act made. We can learn from the hesychastic prayer of the heart how to remember God's presence as often as we can through the use of techniques such as simple ejaculations that center on the name and presence of Jesus.[11] A following chapter will deal with the specific topic of the Jesus Prayer.

But the most beneficial contribution that we can receive from the prayer of the heart for our own personal prayer life is to conceive the prayer of the heart as a way of life in the Trinity. It touches all aspects of the total Christian spiritual life. It touches the whole person, embracing all the means of asceticism and inner discipline, to bring the old man into subjection to Jesus Christ as the new man emerges as a new creation in him (2 Cor 5:17). It is basically contemplation, not *doing* but *being,* an increasing awareness that our true selves are tied intrinsically to God who, as St. Augustine has said, is "more intimate to me than I myself."

It is a never-ending process as we transcend our false ego—our habitual sense, emotional and intellectual programming of God, others and even ourselves to fit into our own rational "boxes"—and descend into the "cave of our heart," that center of freedom where we can experience ourselves flowing out as energy from the Source of all life. It is a nonverbal dialogue in being in which we experience ourselves in the concrete context of our daily lives as tumbling forth from the loving "heart" of God. And in this newfound sense of our unique identity, we can surrender ourselves into the oneness of God.

We may use specific techniques to aid our concentration on the presence of God. The hesychastic Fathers offer us very many techniques, not merely one. A method is good if it works, if it produces the end for which it is used. A German theologian, Johannes Lotz, gives us a prudent guideline in this matter:

> Methods should never be allowed to do violence to our individuality, but they should be used to free it and adapt it for the work of meditation so that each meditator can find his own way.[12]

Techniques are only means to the end of entire Christian life, namely, to return love to God for his infinite love for us in Christ Jesus. But contemplation must always be seen as a gift given to those who earnestly and sincerely seek to receive it by disposing themselves through asceticism. It is an infusion by the Holy Spirit and always remains gratuitous and not dependent upon our works. Thus, in general, the prayer of the heart refers to a constant state whereby we, informed by God's grace, desire to push ourselves to new levels of living in God's presence.

Specifically, the prayer of the heart refers to a level of contemplation that goes beyond the use of images or words. And perhaps in this area we can gain the most profit from the teachings of the Fathers of the desert concerning the prayer of the heart.

DESERT PRAYER

The Fathers of the desert built their whole doctrine of contemplation not around various steps leading to the mystical marriage but rather around a process of our growth under the Holy Spirit into the image and likeness of Jesus Christ. This resemblance to Jesus Christ is not a moral profile but rather a conscious awareness of being one in Christ. It was this state of contemplation in the desert of his heart that allowed St. Paul to cry out, "I live, now, not I, but Christ lives in me!" (Gal 2:20).

We need the encouragement of these athletes of the desert to exhort us to enter into our heart, that inner cell, and not leave it, for it will teach us all we need to know. As the props of sensible consolation, images and words that may have served us earlier in our prayer life drop away from our important values, faith becomes more pure and vibrant. A new presence of God indwelling within us shows itself as darkness. We enter into a necessary dying to our self-reliance and a deepening of faith in God's love that only come when we are in this darkness of the "heart," standing before a wall that is impenetrable by our own intellectual powers.

We cry out for God to show himself in this night of the desert, and we gradually begin to understand our own absolute nothingness before God. Now we must dig roots and at long last opt for God alone! In deep, dark, stark faith we surrender to God as we cry out for his mercy, "Lord, Jesus Christ, Son of God, have mercy on me, a sinner!" This *apophatic* knowledge that is sheer gift from the Holy Spirit to the broken ones, the *Anawim*, in the desert of the heart, is a true knowing by unknowing and has been described by Pseudo-Dionysius who has captured the unanimous doctrine of the desert Fathers:

> . . . and then It (God's presence in darkness) breaks forth, even from the things that are beheld and from those that behold them, and plunges the true initiate into the darkness of unknowing wherein he renounces all the apprehensions of his understanding and is enwrapped in that which is wholly intangible and invisible, belonging wholly to him that is beyond all things and to none else (whether himself or another), and being through the passive stillness of all his reasoning powers united by his highest faculty to Him that is wholly unknowable, of whom thus by a rejection of all knowledge he possesses a knowledge that exceeds his understanding.[13]

The prayer of the heart is the Eastern Christian's way of describing the ongoing process of a human being returning to his or her true state, to a consciousness of being *in Christ*. Through the love received through the Spirit that lives within the divinized human "heart" or consciousness (Rom 5:5), the Christian seeks at all times to live according to that inner dignity ever experienced within the heart in all human relationships and daily events. We live out our baptism, as we cry out to Jesus to release his Spirit of love within our hearts. Through a dynamic process of ongoing purifications and dyings to selfishness, we rise to a more intense, conscious relationship to God. We attain a state of inner harmony and peace, tranquillity and resting in God as our center; this is true *hesychia* or integration into Christ. There is peace and joy in the oneness attained with the indwelling Trinity. There is a burning desire to possess ever more the "absent" God by a stretching out in a willed desire to surrender ourselves more completely, to suffer even more for love of God and neighbor.

THE HEART OF MARY

The Eastern Fathers always had a great devotion to Mary, the *Theotokos* ("Birth-Giver to God"). I believe such devotion kept alive for them the contemplative attitude that they called the prayer of the heart. In Mary they saw the archetype of what every human being, man or woman, and the entire Christian church should be: a wholly integrated being, totally surrendered in faith, obedience and love to the wishes of God.

Erich Neumann, a Jungian analyst, defines the *animus* in every human being as "focused consciousness" while the *anima* is the "diffuse awarenesss."[14] The *anima* is open, receptive, waiting expectantly for new richness in order to absorb it and become ever more its true self. The *anima* describes the prayer of the heart. Jesus exalted it when he preached:

> Unless a wheat grain falls on the ground and dies, it remains on- ly a single grain; but if it dies, it yields a rich harvest. Anyone who loves his life loses it; anyone who hates his life in this world will keep it for the eternal life (Jn 12:24-25).

Mary will always be the sign of the eternal *anima*. She stands as the fulfillment of all human beings. She cries out to all of us in her strong but delicate, tender but enduring, obedience to God's holy will that we become truly human first by develop- ing the *anima* aspect of our nature. She teaches us that we become Christians, not so much when we do something, as when we surrender to the operations of the Holy Spirit to bring forth the Word made flesh, Jesus Christ, both in our lives and in the world around us. The Mary that we are all to become is the integration of our openness to God's free gift of himself into our lives and our *animus* response to return love with love toward our neighbor. The *anima* is where the integration begins as we let go of the controlled consciousness that we hold over our lives and surrender in complete poverty to God's gift of himself as grace.

St. Luke refers twice in his Gospel to the heart of Mary in a sense similar to the use of the word by the hesychastic Fathers. At Bethlehem she reflects on the words of the shepherds, "As for Mary, she treasured all these things and pondered them in her heart" (Lk 2:19). Her life with Jesus at Nazareth is summarized in similar words, "His mother stored up all these things in her heart" (Lk 2:51). Mary's heart, that focal point of deepest personalized consciousness, was always centered on Jesus, the Word. She becomes the mother of God only in order to surrender as the lowly handmaid of the Lord (Lk 1:46). She pondered every happening of her Son in the light of the Holy Spirit.

Her whole life was a life lived in her "heart" where she encountered the loving activity of God through his Word and the Holy Spirit. As she lived only to let that Word come forth into new life and to give that Word of life to others, so she continues in glory to pray the prayer of the heart, a total life of a totally integrated Christian in whom God has conquered every level of being. Mary, the contemplative on earth and now in glory, is the loving servant of the Lord. Love received makes it possible for her to give of that love to others. It makes her hunger in her heart, with perfect purity of heart, to give of herself in loving service to the whole world, to every human being made according to the image and likeness of her Son. Mary becomes for us the completely realized, integrated human being. The contemplative in action is the virgin mother of the Word of God, receiving and sharing that Divine Life with the whole world.

This is the meaning and the application of the prayer of the heart for us moderns. It is a state of continuously becoming integrated as fulfilled Christians by living in the *heart* the death-resurrection of Jesus Christ. The measure of the degree of integration attained by us and by the Fathers of the desert must always be measured by the love and humility shown in service toward others. This is what the prayer of the heart is really all about.

4.

BROKENNESS UNTO LIFE

The Christian life has been described by Jesus Christ and his disciples as a death-unto-life experience. He described this life as a denial of one's self, as a shouldering of one's cross and following him (Mt 10:38; 16:24; Mk 8:34; Lk 9:23; 14:27). Jesus insisted that the seed had to fall into the earth and *die* before it could bring forth greater fruit (Jn 12:24). Nicodemus was told by Jesus that he had to be reborn from above (Jn 3:4).

But this is to describe the law of inner growth in all human lives. We, beings made according to God's own image and likeness (Gn 1:26), possess the ability to *stretch* ourselves upward to attain new levels of transcendent meaningfulness by letting go of lower levels of being. Holy Scripture presents this conversion process in terms of an *exodus,* a passing-over from a state of slavery in Egypt into the state of becoming progressively free in the darkness and sterility of the desert that leads to the Promised Land.

Psychologists speak of it as a twofold movement. The first stage consists in accepting ourselves with honesty and without excuse. This is an awakening moment, revealing the truth that what we thought was our true personhood was in reality a *false* self. Many of us seek various ways of escaping this self-knowledge, such as great busyness with work or travel.

Only if we learn to accept our existential self sincerely can we ever hope to open up to the second movement, namely, to hunger and thirst in the totality of our being to be someone more noble, more loving, more good. This is the elan toward new life. It can only follow the letting go of the false self and all the protective devices and techniques we have been using to secure the lie that that person is our true self. And how most of us human beings detest the thought of the dying process that will yield to new life!

Paul Tillich writes in his book, *The Courage to Be:* "Actualization of being implies the ability to take courageously upon oneself the anxiety of nonbeing."[1] It is this anxiety and fear of letting go of our "Linus blanket" of pseudo-security that we all resist in the beginning stages of a conversion of ourselves toward God and toward our true person in his Word. To split this hard shell of self-containment and control over ourselves, over others and even over God is the harrowing first step into new life.

This conversion experience can also be described in terms of prayer, for every true conversion to living according to more transcendent values can come about only through the ultimate loving power that allows us to let go and surrender ourselves into his caring hands. The French spiritual writer, Denis Vasse, defines prayer as the passage from need to desire.[2] In the initial stages of prayer we needed God, but we created God according to our own images. He was to satisfy all of our creaturely needs and, in fact, help us retain that false self we lived with for so many years.

The transitional point comes when we can look earnestly at ourselves and begin to accept the fact that there is something false, unreal, unauthentic in the way we approach God, in the way we look at ourselves and at others. In the words of Gabriel Marcel, such a person "has become once and for all a question for himself."[3] The basic question we need to ask ourselves is: Will we stay inside ourselves, groping for ways in which we can let God be truly God instead of running "outside" to be diverted from the call to new life? Marcel describes the feeling of inner emptiness that comes to the person who courageously looks inside:

> When we are at rest, we find ourselves almost inevitably put in the presence of our own inner emptiness, and this very emptiness is in reality intolerable to us. But there is more, there is the

fact that through this emptiness we inevitably become aware of the misery of our condition, a "condition so miserable," says Pascal, "that nothing can console us when we think about it carefully." Hence the necessity of diversion.[4]

BREAKING THE IDOLS

By staying "inside" and exploring ourselves on deeper levels than we usually seek, we begin to develop a distaste for our false self. We see the many shams and deceits we have been employing in order to put off accepting the call to new life. We see the false posturing and the little tricks we use to push ourselves forward before others, to impress them with our worth by displaying the things that we have done.

Above all, the emptiness within reveals in an amazing burst of light inside of darkness how dishonest we have been toward God in our prayer. We see how we have hidden behind doctrines and liturgical rituals—structures of our religious or spiritual life that served to guarantee both a false security, and a closing off to God's call to conversion. Now, through a deepening of faith we have the courage to look at our habitual attitude toward God. Shame fills our hearts at the brazenness of how we used God for our own selfish purposes. Need, not true love, was behind most of our prayer life. Now prayer becomes a desire to crash down the false idols, the images and words used to present ourselves to God as though we were his equals, or worse, that he was at our beck and call.

The working of God's grace to instill into us anxiety, fear and disgust as we confront our existence in the light of our "nonbeing" is not merely a self-centered reflection on death. It is an ontological "nostalgia" to leave the "husks of swine" and return to our true selves. It is to be in love with our heavenly Father in total self-surrendering.

THE DESERT FATHERS

The athletes of the spiritual life who show us performances

of courage and constancy in facing their false self and doing the "inner battle" to allow God total freedom in their lives are the desert Fathers. They lived continually in the dialectical tension of darkness and light, of death and resurrection to a new life in Christ. St. Symeon the New Theologian (+1022) rather dramatically and poetically describes what he found when he came to grips with his false self:

> Likewise that soul about which I am speaking,
> when it sees how the light shines
> and knows that itself is completely in most terrible darkness
> and in this completely enclosed prison
> of most profound ignorance,
> then it sees just where it is lying,
> where it is locked in
> and that this place is completely a mudhole,
> full of slimy, poisonous snakes:
> that it itself is chained,
> both hands and feet bound by shackles
> and that it is covered with dust and filth;
> that it is also wounded
> from the bites of the reptiles
> and that its own flesh is puffed up
> and also covered with numerous worms.
> Seeing this, how will the soul not shudder?
> How will it not weep?
> And how will it not cry out?
> And ardently be repentant and beg to be rescued
> from such terrible fetters?
> Yes, all who see such
> indeed will lament and groan
> and will want to follow after Christ
> who makes the light so radiant![5]

SIN AND COMPUNCTION

The Fathers of the desert dared to break the idols that they had built up for themselves in prayer and stretched into the desert of their brokenness. Miles and miles of uninterrupted aridity and sterility both within and without kept them crying out for the mercy and healing power of their living God. They faced their own inner resistance, rebellion and anger against a God who dared to rule completely in their lives. They discovered that they were one with a whole world in rebellion against their Maker. As they strove constantly to become pure in heart they could cry out that it was still not sufficient. "What man can say, 'I have cleansed my heart, I am purified of my sin'?" (Prv 20:9). Yet they knew that their duty was to cry out incessantly: "Have mercy on me, O God, in your goodness, in your great tenderness wipe away my faults; wash me clean of my guilt, purify me from my sin" (Ps 51:1-2).

Much in the writings of the early Fathers on the spiritual life must be demythologized. When we are able to enter into their specialized, linguistic symbols—symbols that express a greater experience than any word-for-word translation can yield to us—perhaps then we will be able to see more clearly the substantial truths that are as applicable to our spiritual lives as they were to the lives of such early Christians.

One very evident and essential teaching stressed by all the early Fathers, one that remains applicable for us moderns when all the necessary demythologizing has been done, is their doctrine on sin and compunction. They saw sin as more than a mere action, a legal violation of an extrinsic law. It was a contagion that permeated everything they touched, saw, smelled, heard and tasted. Like David the penitent, the Fathers of the desert knew that in a very real way they were conceived in sin (Ps 51:5). There were some sins that they were convinced were deliberate offenses against the commands of God. Other sins crippled them as a dark cloud of ignorance that kept them in disobedience to God's command to be attentive to the evil forces around them.

They saw weeping for their sins as a necessary obligation for any Christian. "Happy those who mourn: they shall be comforted" (Mt 5:5) was Christ's exhortation and, therefore, it became that also of Origen, Ephraim, Basil, Gregory Nazianzen, Gregory of Nyssa, John Chrysostom and Isaac the Syrian. In a word, this is the common doctrine of all the early Christian ascetics and mystics.

PENTHOS

The early monks fled into the desert where, reduced literally to only the barest necessities for maintaining life, they purified themselves from all attachments in order to listen to God in the clear, pure air that is found only in deep silence and solitude. In Holy Scripture they found the basis for what they considered a divine command, "to mourn according to God." The Old Testament uses the Greek word *penthos* 120 times to indicate the grief experienced by those in public or private mourning. Isaiah announced God's desire "to comfort all those who mourn and to give them for ashes a garland, for mourning robe the oil of gladness" (Is 61:3).[6]

Irénée Hausherr, one of the great authorities on Byzantine spirituality, defines compunction *(penthos)* as: "Sorrow at the prospect of losing eternal salvation on the part of ourselves or of others."[7] More than a rational concept, compunction was an experience, more or less permanent, given to the repentant sinner by God in his condescending mercy. Joel's words formed the basis of the early monks' renewed conversion or *metanoia:* "Come back to me with all your heart, fasting, weeping, mourning. Let your hearts be broken, not your garments torn, turn to Yahweh your God again, for he is all tenderness and compassion, slow to anger, rich in graciousness, and ready to relent" (Jl 2:12-13).

OBSTACLES TO A SORROWING HEART

For the desert Fathers cultivating a lively sense of compunction was an absolute necessity for every Christian. It fostered the conditions of brokenness and the insights into the sinfulness and precariousness of human existence. They saw, therefore, that any neglect of spiritual exercises such as frequent examination of conscience, serious meditation on the words and life of Christ along with his stress of man's end and judgment unto eternal reward or punishment would cause a corresponding insensitivity in the human heart and open it to a spirit of dissipation. Pride would dominate such a "worldly" life, while compunction would foster the growth of humility, which would bring true knowledge of God's allness and of man as sheer gift of God's goodness.

Excessive looseness in speech was considered one of the main avenues of dissipation that, in the words of St. Dorotheus, begets all other vices.[8] In fact, any excess or immoderation, which in itself indicates a self-centeredness and a failure to refer to God as the measure of proper conduct, had to be avoided. This held also in the teaching of the desert Fathers in liturgical matters where elaborate chants and preoccupation with nonessentials could dry the heart of the monk and take him away from his true occupation of adoring God through clear knowledge of God and knowledge of himself. Overspeculation in a dry, rationalistic manner on theological problems was another danger to compunction since it tended to make the theologian proud and created a God too much according to a human model.

AIDS TO COMPUNCTION

Thoughts that dwelt on the individual's past infidelities toward so loving a God, on the "existential" awareness of human weakness and a propensity toward evil and hence on the possibility of an eternity separated from God, effected a movement away from self-love toward a passionate love of God. True conversion as a constant state of stretching out toward God, of submitting always to God as the end of one's life, brings a period of revolt and distaste. At the root of all these negative drives is pride, an unwillingness to acknowledge total dependence on God's love. The only means of countering this profound bondage is to desire and yearn for humility, the serene acceptance that one's life belongs to God.

Praxis or the ascetical life began with "sitting in one's cell" so that he would learn everything that he needed to know. In a serious centering upon God and reflecting upon ultimate concern of what awaits one in eternal judgment, the Christian would be led to an interior state of sorrow, of weeping for past sins, of weeping for new strength to be found only in God's loving mercy.

THE GIFT OF TEARS

The gift of tears was seen by the Fathers as a concrete criterion of their intense sorrow which necessarily, if it were real, would have repercussions throughout the whole body. Compunction gave a sense of self-identity in a person's relationship to God and in this experienced unity tears flowed forth as a register of a sorrow that touched the person on the deepest level. John Climacus writes in his seventh step: "Groanings and sorrows cry to the Lord. Tears shed from fear intercede for us; but tears of all-holy love show us that our prayer has been accepted."[9]

Evagrius in his treatise on prayer exhorts monks:

> Pray first for the gift of tears so that by means of sorrow you may soften your native rudeness. Then having confessed your sins to the Lord, you may receive from him the remission of sins. Pray with tears and your request will find a hearing. Nothing so gratifies the Lord as supplication offered in the midst of tears.[10]

At some unanticipated point in this process of experiencing one's interior brokenness and alienation from God, one's hardness of heart through years of bitterness and hatred, and one's pride and indifference to God's loving call to share his happiness and life, the individual at last has an experience of a heart of stone being replaced by a heart of flesh (Ez 36:26).

Tears of grief burst forth from the depths of the inner being, the heart, which has been so long living in deceit, anxieties and the fear of death.

The Fathers were not concerned with excessive hysteria. They were seeking in tears primarily a psychological state of persuasion that touched them, not on any one level of sense or emotion or mind, but rather at the core of their being. They distrusted any degree of interior compunction that did not also manifest itself in a reaction that flowed from their inner "core" outwardly into their senses. They surely had met neurotic persons who wept tears in abundance as Climacus states:

> I have seen small tear drops shed with difficulty like drops of blood and I have also seen fountains of tears poured out without difficulty. And I judged those toilers more by their toil than by their tears, and I think that God does too.[11]

They also knew tears could measure the interior compunction when the total person was deeply moved by sorrow, as Climacus adds that "tears are the product of thought and the father of thought is a rational mind."[12] The Fathers applied to the spiritual life the same experience had in one's natural relationships to others, for if a person were to experience a great sorrow, regret, fear of losing the most precious possession in life, that person would show this deeply felt emotion by tears.[13] The desire to be penetrated with as deep a sorrow as possible before the goodness of God was the important feature stressed. The interior desire in itself was a spiritual weeping that, the desert Fathers felt, would turn to physical tears as a gift of God when they reached an intense and abiding sense of compunction. Compunction itself deeply experienced was the important goal to be attained. The gift of tears was never desired as a separate "charism" in itself or for the consolation it would bring the penitent.

Isaac the Syrian best articulates this doctrine of compunction and the added gift of tears. He teaches that the first manifestation of tears is a crying out in the darkness, a thirsting so strong for healing and eternal salvation that tears flow from an honest appraisal of oneself. Humility, as a gifted insight given by God, manifests itself in lamentation for the condition of bondage which affects not only the individual but the entire human race. St. Gregory of Nyssa writes, "It is impossible for one to live without tears who considers things exactly as they really are. . . ."[14]

Tears were the signs of labor before a new life was born. Grace is about to bring forth the Divine Image into the light of the life to come. But tears of sorrow give way to a higher level of spiritual insight and growth in divine life. The accent is no longer on the dark self as tears of grief yield to tears of mercy and love. St. Isaac describes this level of spiritual growth:

> Then by them (tears of grief) the gate leading to the second order will not be opened by him, an order which is far superior, because it contains the sign of the receiving of mercy. Those tears which have their origin in insight make the body shake; they flow spontaneously and compulsion has no share in them. They also anoint the body and the aspect of the face is changed. For a joyful heart renders the body beautiful. These tears moisten the whole face when the mind lives in solitude. The body acquires by them as it were some sustenance and joy is diffused over the face.[15]

Tears were a sign of a second baptism, this time not by water but by the Holy Spirit.[16] Experiencing profoundly the infinite mercy and love of God for the Christian, the individual experiences also a liberating joy, peace and merciful love toward the entire world. Having wept for his sins, he truly is comforted by God as Jesus had taught. Purified of all inordinate, passionate desires, the Fathers of the desert knew a permanently abiding sense of tranquillity that begot interior happiness. It was neither the absence of trouble through a blind resignation to God's providence, as found so often in Muslim asceticism, nor a philosophical stoicism that simply ignored the rest of the world.

This interior happiness was at the basis of the Christian experience: through the cross to light. Compunction was the dy-

ing process and joy was the resurrection of all one's powers into a
new life that produced a hundredfold in peace and happiness.
Now the Spirit has poured deeper faith, hope and love of God
into one's heart. God indwells as a "consuming fire" and such
burning love cannot but release tears, no longer bitter, but now
joyful. This becomes an advanced state of pure prayer, as St.
Isaac describes it:

> Every time when the thought of God is stirred in his spirit, the
> heart will become hot with love at once, the eyes will shed
> multitudinous tears; for love is accustomed to shed tears at the
> recollection of the beloved. He that is in this state will never be
> found destitute of tears, because he is never without abundant
> recollection of God, so that even during sleep he speak with
> him. Love is accustomed to practice these things and this is the
> accomplishment of man is this life.[17]

What the desert Fathers universally experienced through
the gift of tears was a cosmic oneness in love and mercy not only
toward all other human beings but toward animals, plants and
all inanimate creation. God's loving presence shines through all
of creation as a self-giving in love that can only engender in the
heart of the purified contemplative a like response of love and
mercy toward the whole world. Such a heart, freed from all taint
of narcissism through tears, can look upon all human beings
with the eyes of the compassionate God. The heart finds itself
"full of mercy for all mankind" and is "afflicted with pity for
them and burns as with fire without personal discrimination,"
as St. Isaac writes.[18]

Such universal love for all mankind is exemplified by the
hermit Agathon, who cared for six months for a sick man whom
he had found abandoned on the streets. "I wished that I could
find a leper and give him my body and take his—this is perfect
love; let us resemble our Fathers, that we may be thought wor-
thy of grace, as they were."[19]

The Pilgrim in the Russian classic, *The Way of a Pilgrim*,
reflects this constant experience of the Fathers who learned to
weep tears and through the gift of tears learned to pray always in

their hearts, when he expresses his oneness with all creatures:

> The whole outside world . . . seemed to me full of charm and delight. Everything drew me to love and thank God: people, trees, plants, animals. I saw them all as my kinsfolk, I found in all of them the magic of the name of Jesus.[20]

INTERPRETATION

There has been a loss of teaching and practice of an abiding sense of sorrow for sins and an experience of our interior brokenness and alienation in modern Western Christianity. This loss has been pointed out by such spiritual writers as Dom Marmion, F. Faber, I. Hausherr and P. Regamey.[21] To us, dwelling on sorrow for sins seems quite negative, even gruesome; certainly not very self-fulfilling. Perhaps we have not really understood true compunction, especially as the early Fathers of the desert did. We tend to fear sheer emotionalism, to say nothing of hysteria. A plethora of studies done on religious aberrations has made us suspicious of anything not rooted in sound reason. But we may be losing a means that could help us to remain in a more constant state of compunction, itself an aid to remaining reverently and lovingly in the presence of God in constant prayer.

Paul Tillich, in a short essay entitled "The Eternal Now," shows how repentance is more than a feeling of sorrow about wrong actions. "It is the act of the whole person in which he separates himself from elements of his being, discarding them into the past as something that no longer has any power over the present."[22] When we begin to live more consciously and more interiorly, we make contact with what St. Paul described as "sin which lives inside my body" (Rom 7:23). Sin becomes something more than acts that transgress a divine law. The Fathers had passed beyond the extrinsic aspects of the law and had entered into a deep self-knowledge of the inner movements of the "heart" as well as a deep consciousness of God's very immediate and tender love for them. In a word, sin for them was anything that was an obstacle to joyfully living the message of the Paschal Mystery. And insofar as they knew such sin, they realized the need to take responsibility for it by crying out forgiveness in order to receive the healing mercy of God's love into deeper and deeper levels of consciousness.

For many centuries Western theologians placed the accent of sin on the act or on the vice or disposition formed by repeated actions. St. Theophan the Recluse gives three meanings to sin: a culpable deed; a passion; a state of soul or an interior disposition.[23] St. John's Gospel describes sin as a state—a permanent, interior disposition. Not only man individually but the entire "world" is in sin (Jn 1:29). St. Paul personifies sin that has entered into the world. Similar expressions are found in the Oriental writers. Macarius writes:

> For us, however, evil is real since it inhabits in our heart and there it operates by suggesting wicked and obscene thoughts and by not allowing us to pour out pure prayers. It leads our mind into captivity to this world. It has put on our souls and has touched all our bones and members.[24]

Yet the Fathers, using the biblical personification of sin, were quite aware that moral evil was a deprivation of being within the free person. One insight that they give us is their understanding of any irregular movement within the heart as an impurity and something for which they were obligated to seek inner healing. They do not confuse in their writings the difference between voluntary and involuntary sins. But they place maximum responsibility on the individual for the condition of his or her heart. Sin for them was always the work of human freedom, either in the actual choosing to do what is wrong or in the choosing not to resist the movements from within that, by a lack of inner attention, would lead to sinning.

True wisdom, tied to contemplation, for the Fathers consisted in perceiving the inner *logos* of each creature as ultimately related to God's *Logos*. Not to be attentive to such inner harmony in each creature would be to sin by omission. Such ignorance of God's plan would result from disobedience to God's command to love God and neighbor in all things.

EFFECTS OF SIN

Rather than concentrate on the exterior effect of evil actions, the Fathers of the desert stressed the interior perversion introduced into the heart. Many of the Fathers would follow St. Basil's teaching that deemphasized the distinction between objectively grave and venial sin and emphasized rather that every transgression of God's law is "one and the same" transgression.[25] Thus something can be "grave" even if the external act seemingly was without importance. What would determine the gravity would be the degree of self-indulgence and attachment to one's own desires and the turning away from God.

The consequence of sin, therefore, is that it obscures the image of God in man. Sin is darkness that covers over the spiritual eyes of the soul, preventing the Christian from seeing God everywhere. Such disorder and lack of harmony have an impact on the entire world. The social aspect and cosmic dimension of sin can be seen in Russian spirituality that posits a relationship between earth and man's good or bad relationship to God, his fellow man and the rest of creation.

Dostoyevsky captures this ancient Russian insight, dating probably from pagan times, when he describes earth as a holy mother that a human being can offend, soil and perpetrate evil against. Aloysha, the monk-novice in *The Brothers Karamazov*, bends down to whisper his sinful deeds into the bowels of the earth as he seeks reconciliation with the cosmic harmony that he supposedly upset by his sins. No one, according to the Fathers of the East, ever could sin individually or "privately." Cosmic vibrations are set up that demand a forgiveness.

CRY FOR MERCY

We have seen above the teaching of the Fathers on the necessity of crying out in true sorrow for any sin in order that God give the sinner forgiveness and healing mercy. Compunction for the early Fathers of the desert and for all Christians who have grasped their insights is the means the Christian uses to live in the "eternal now" while living also in a past, present, future continuum. God, for the Fathers who wept "because there was no other way to perfection,"[26] was not a goal, an object toward which they moved and which they attained only upon death. God is the abundance of love, the overflowing of his uncreated energies that bombards his creatures at every moment. Human beings, made to his image and drawn to the intimate relationship of a loving child to a loving father, not only in the past have freely turned away from greater growth by sin, but in the present and in the future feel the pull within and all around of a world that is "groaning in travail" (Rom 8:22) until it reaches its perfection in Christ. This "existential angst" cries out for Another, One who lies beyond the ravages of time and space, One who is the possessor of all perfections.

All one had to do, the Fathers were convinced, was to cry out to this merciful Father who so loved the human race that he gave his only Son to die for us in order that we might have eternal life (Jn 3:16). And such forgiving mercy was easily available. All one had to do was to cry out with sincerity and God would do the rest. St. John Chrysostom frequently in his homilies exhorts his audience: "Have you sinned? Tell God: 'I have sinned.' Is that very difficult?"[27] And yet St. Theophan the Recluse insisted that to admit "I am a sinner" is more important than "I have sinned."[28] Out of this conviction of the necessity of confessing a constant state of being locked into sin as sinners, of always needing the mercy of God, a mercy that will be readily granted to them who confess publicly in the liturgy or privately in their own prayers, grew the insistent litanies for mercy and the Jesus Prayer: "Lord Jesus Christ, Son of God, have mercy on me, a sinner."

But in the universal teaching of the early Eastern Fathers, it is compunction, that abiding sorrow for the godless past and the fear of a future without God, that allows the Christian to contact God. God gives himself to the weak, the poor, the needy; in a word, to the humble because they have entered into an experiential knowledge of their creaturehood. The desert Fathers, crying incessantly with the penitent David, ''. . . wash me clean of my guilt, purify me from my sin'' (Ps 51:2), experienced a second baptism. Climacus writes, ''But sins committed after baptism are washed away by tears.''[29] In this freedom from guilt, the desert Christian of true compunction gazed more clearly on the beauty and goodness of God. Filled with great tenderness and longing for greater union with God, he found his strength in his weakness. His strength was in the all-powerful Father whom he experienced mostly in God's tender forgiveness of his weaknesses.

APPLICATION

We can ask ourselves whether such constant accent on our brokenness and sinfulness is not overly morose and negative. Does it not denigrate the death and resurrection of Jesus Christ as the power that has taken away our sinfulness and established us as children of God's very own triune family?

Dr. Karl Menninger, of the Menninger Foundation in Topeka, Kansas, was once convinced, through his treatment of psychotic patients, that the stress on sin, as taught by many Christian preachers, had a greatly negative and unhealthy effect upon many Christians. Later, however, he wrote a book entitled: *Whatever Became of Sin?*[30] He laments in this work the disappearance of both the recognition of our sins as sins and the taking of the responsibility for our sins to expiate the guilt incurred. He defines sin: ''Sin has a willful, defiant or disloyal quality; *someone* is defied or offended or hurt. The willful disregard or sacrifice of the welfare of others for the welfare or satisfaction of the self is an essential quality of the concept sin.

. . . And sin is thus, at heart, a refusal of the love of others.''[31]

His thesis revolves around the necessity for all of us human beings to recognize our guilt in so many of the violations of injustice toward the poor and suffering in the world, in times past as well as in the present. All human acts, he insists, are both voluntary and involuntary. Many of the sins that place at the door of our unconscious much guilt are collective sins. All of us are in one way or another responsible and guilty for the injustices against the North American Indians, the conditions of society, environmental pollution, sloth, lack of concern for the poverty throughout the world and the increase of destructive war weapons.

This universal guilt is something real, deeply embedded within our consciousness and our unconscious. One author describes it:

> We are oppressed by the inevitability of wars which break out like ulcers, though nearly everybody is against them; by the natural arrogance of capitalism and colonialism; by the poisoning of the atmosphere by racial and class hatred. Six million men perished in gas chambers on the highly civilized continent of Europe. Our selfish incapacity to love one another, our failure to change our life and thinking is part and parcel of all this. We too do harm to men. We play our part in the great evil of the world. Our hands are too clean.[32]

When we viewed God, the world and ourselves in a very static manner, sin was easily taken care of as a deliberate action against a law of God. But we failed to consider the first sin of Adam and Eve as a part of our ongoing sinfulness. We are caught in a universal contagion of sin that is always exerting its evil web of selfishness around us and strangling the love-power of God's life within us. Holy Scripture teaches us and the Fathers of the desert cry out to us that we all sin, that we are in a condition of spiritual darkness and sickness. It is love that makes us healthy human beings and we are constantly being impeded from living a life of love toward every human being that we meet.

Scholars, such as S. Lyonnet, S.J., and Piet Schoonenberg, S.J., point out that in St. Paul's doctrine about "original sin," we are all tied, not by some legalistic tie through birth into the human race, but by our very human personal sins that are indeed a part of that original sin and whose evil we add into a universe that continues to resist God's love.[33] Bernard Haring, C.Ss. R., describes our sinfulness in neglecting to make this world a more equitable world for all. In a static view of morality neither the evil and guilt of this sin nor the need to repent and reform could have been seen. He writes:

> If we do not participate actively in the shaping of a healthier public opinion, a healthier way of life—in housing, economic opportunity, and so on—and fail to work to improve our social institutions, we are deciding to remain in our sinfulness and thereby to increase sinfulness in the world. We decidedly remain sinners and relinquish our hope for the Messianic peace if we do not work for reconciliation and peace on all levels. Equally, whoever refuses to his fellow men a proportionate share in responsibility and coresponsibility for the physical, social, cultural, and ecclesiastical life is increasing the sinfulness of the world.[34]

Besides our deliberate sins and deliberate omissions, there are multitudes of obstacles that prevent us from even looking at the omissions and taking responsibility for our sinfulness. These, too, are part of the sinfulness that needs crying out to God for mercy and healing. All these things—our past habits, sins, thought patterns; our training and education; our parents and family life; our life in a country at any given period of history with all the doubtful decisions and sinfulness found in all levels of government, in the industrial world, in the armed forces—exert upon us a constant pressure from the past. How bound we are with lack of forgiveness and with prejudices toward others! What fears control us daily and prevent us from living under the law of Christ's love! Fears of the past, fears of the future, fears of the next moment urge us to actions or inaction that prevents the grace of Christ from operating in our lives and producing the fruit of the Holy Spirit that is chiefly love (Gal 5:16-22).

INTERIOR WEEPING

All of us human beings, regardless of the time and place in which we live, should know through experience that the closer we approach the beauty and holiness of God, the more aware we become of the darkness and sinfulness within our own hearts. We readily see the scattered, dried bones of what could have been strewn over the haunting memories of our past. As we look upon the mountain of God's infinite love for each of us, we see the valley of our own nothingness. God's unbounded presence as love shows how tightly constrained we are within the prison of our selfishness and egoism. If we have the courage to turn within and, and in silence and honesty, look into the tomb of our inner darkness, the light of God's tender love illumines us, ever so softly and healingly and interior tears well up in our spiritual eyes. We whisper in the depths of our heart, "Have mercy on me, O God, in Your goodness" (Ps 51:1).

In such inner quieting we gently yield to the operations of the Holy Spirit who shows us what needs continual healing from deep within us. We see our fragmentation and we sorrow at seeing what could have been. We feel caught in a prison of darkness and yet we can see a delicate ray of light leading us through the crack of *metanoia,* conversion to the Lord Jesus. The words of Joel were not meant only for the Israelites but also for us:

> . . . .come back to me with all your heart,
> fasting, weeping, mourning.
> Let your hearts be broken, not your garments torn,
> turn to Yahweh your God again,
> for he is all tenderness and compassion,

slow to anger, rich in graciousness,
and ready to relent (Jl 2:12-13).

As we sit within our inner desert like the desert Fathers of earlier centuries, we learn to yield to the indwelling presence of Jesus Christ, the Divine Physician, who alone can bring life and that life more abundantly. We cry out as often as we can, day and night, with distrust in our powers to save ourselves, but with childlike trust in Jesus the Healer: "Lord, Jesus Christ, Son of God, have mercy on me, a sinner." This demands a life of reflection, of sensitive inner knowledge in the light of God's indwelling presence and infinite love. In his light we see our darkness.

In that darkness we honestly recognize our guilt and sinfulness. We move far beyond mere actions to understand by the power of the Holy Spirit our brokenness and our constant need of God's forgiving, healing love. The deeper our sorrow through the Spirit's illumination, the stronger our wish to freely surrender to the dominance of God. We are living our baptism on a deeper level, a continued second baptism in the Spirit. We are dying to self-centeredness through interior weeping to rise to a new life in the Risen Jesus Christ.

ONE WITH A BROKEN WORLD

As we enter through compunction into an inner healing through the love of the Spirit poured out into our heart (Rom 5:5), we know the joy of being one with the heavenly Father. This unity of "one Spirit, one body" and "one God who is Father of all, over all, through all and with all" (Eph 4:4-6) allows us to remember our brothers and sisters who do not know the Father's love for them. Like Jesus weeping over Jerusalem, we hold our hands up to the heavenly Father and cry out because of the hard hearts of family members, relatives, friends, countrymen, fellow human beings scattered in all parts of the world. We put on the broken heart of the God-Man who gave his life that all human beings might have eternal life. Like Jesus, we too wish to gather them all under wings of caring love, but they would not (Mt 23:37).

We learn to pray but also to fast as we stand poor before the throne of God and beg mercy for our fellow human beings. "Tears flood my eyes night and day, unceasingly, since a crushing blow falls on the daughter of my people, a most grievous injury" (Jer 14:17). It is no longer that they are sinful and pitiful persons and we are saved and want them to be saved also. Now by the Spirit's revelation, we experience the *oneness* in brokenness and sinfulness that we share with our brothers and sisters. We so associate with sinners that we consider ourselves as the author of their evil, confessing to God and falling down before him in great affliction. We burn with a love that all human beings might know God more perfectly. We plead with God that we might suffer punishment in their place.

Such a oneness in true Christian brotherhood with the whole human race, with individual members that are hurting and living miserably on any level of body, soul or spirit, calls out a constant sense of compassion and mercy for all. It is the most practical approach to inner freedom and freedom to create a better world. Father Zossima in Dostoyevsky's *The Brothers Karamazov* expresses the secret of the transformation of this world:

> To transform the world, to recreate it afresh, man must turn into another path psychologically. Until you have become, in actual fact, a brother to everyone, brotherhood will not come to pass. No sort of scientific teaching, no kind of common interest, will ever teach man to share property and privilege with equal consideration for all.[35]

INNER FREEDOM

Through such individual and corporate sense of compunction and brokenness we become weak. We surrender at each moment to the indwelling Holy Spirit and his promptings. Hardness of heart yields through a repentant spirit to a willingness to listen and a promptitude into doing whatsover God commands. "Speak, Yahweh, your servant is listening" (1 Sm 3:10). In such inner humility, living every thought, word and action before God and fellow human beings, we enter into a newfound freedom. We are freed of the greatest enemy, the false self. It no longer has the power to create its own world according to our selfish needs. Now the love of God has cleansed our hearts and we live on a new plateau of oneness with the mind of God and all creatures.

Such freedom to take life totally into our hands and to submit it freely and joyfully back to the heavenly Father floods our whole being with inner peace and joy, the true signs of the fruit of the Spirit (Gal 5:22). These radiate as soft lights that go out to dispel the darkness in the lives of others. There is a childlike exuberance toward life. Each day brings new ways of living dynamically according to the newly released powers of love that had lain there for so long in a dormant state. Jesus Christ dwells within with his resurrectional victory. Nothing can separate us from him, our Rock and our Salvation. His name and presence are constantly on our lips and in our hearts. For he promised that all who would mourn would be comforted (Mt 5:4). And even when others would persecute us for his sake, we find it easy to rejoice and be glad for a rich reward awaits us in heaven (Mt 5:10).

A strange alchemy exists between sorrow for sins and the joy that flows from the realized experience of dying and rising, of being transfigured to glory in Jesus Christ. This joy no one can take from us. It is a joy that Jesus Christ learned by weeping for the sins of the world and begging forgiveness of the Father for the ignorance of all mankind. On the cross he experienced this joy as he freely surrendered his whole life in death for love of all of us.

A CONSTANT NEED

Much is outdated and needs demythologizing in the writings of these fiercely serious Christians of an earlier age who wept for their sins and the sins of the entire world. But one truth will always remain the same, both for the monk in the Egyptian desert of the fourth century and for the Christian of the cybernetic society of the 20th century. We all have need of the baptism of Jesus Christ, received not once, but over and over, whereby we are washed clean of more and more of our deep traces of resistance to God's love. But we receive the saving waters of baptism only if we cry out constantly. We are in continual need of God's recreating force in our lives. And yet God is always the forgiving Lover, ready to burst into our meaningless flow of consciousness in time with his meaningful presence that allows us to make of *now* the eternal *Now* of God.

5.

THE SPIRITUAL COMBAT

Salvation or the sharing in God's triune life is a sheer gift from God to us. St. Paul writes: "Because it is by grace that you have been saved, through faith; not by anything of your own, but by a gift from God; not by anything that you have done, so that nobody can claim the credit" (Eph 2:8).

God gratuitously pledges himself to a covenanted love with each of us individually and with all of us communally as his chosen people. Yet we must respond to his call. We have seen this as a call to conversion, a passing over from our using God for our own self-centered needs to a total surrender of ourselves to please him in all things. Moreover, we saw what sin meant within us and outside of us. We learned the important lesson of constantly crying out to God for his mercy in order that we may be healed.

Now let us turn to that aspect of our spiritual life that in the concrete spells out what we must do to effect a continual response to God's call to share his life. The Eastern Fathers have often been misunderstood by Westerners, especially ones like St. Jerome who thought that all Oriental Christians were Pelagians who believed that they could lift themselves up to heaven by their own efforts. The Fathers of the desert realized that there would be no gifts of contemplation *(theoria)* unless concomitantly there was a continued response, a readiness to embrace the life of *praxis* or the ascetical life of, negatively, uprooting any immoderate self-love and, positively, putting on the mind of Christ by developing all of the Christian virtues.

INVISIBLE BATTLE

The lives of the desert Fathers show us one outstanding feature: They continually sought to push themselves to greater levels of interiority. Unlike the majority of human beings, they placed their priority of time and attention upon the interior life, for they knew that it was in the heart that the contest was to be decided: to love and serve God or Mammon. Taking their inspiration from Jesus Christ himself, they journeyed inward and purified their hearts so that the kingdom of God would be established completely. Jesus had told them:

> What goes into the mouth does not make a man unclean; it is what comes out of the mouth that makes him unclean (Mt 15:11).

> You who clean the outside of cup and dish and leave the inside full of extortion and intemperance. Blind Pharisee! Clean the inside of cup and dish first so that the outside may become clean as well (Mt 23:25-26).

The Fathers, therefore, using St. Paul's language, view the spiritual life for all Christians as an invisible battle *(aoratos polemos)*. This battle has to be waged by ourselves with God's graces through Christ Jesus against invisible enemies. Our whole spiritual welfare now and for all eternity depends on the way we wage this battle against the common enemy of all mankind, the demons. This war is fought both in the body and the soul. But it is in the heart or the mind that the battlefield is marked off and where victory or defeat is decided.

St. Paul warns all Christians and the Fathers use similar language:

> Put God's armor on so as to be able to resist the devil's tactics. For it is not against human enemies that we have to struggle, but against the sovereignties and the powers who originate the darkness in this world, the spiritual army of evil in the heavens (Eph 6:11-12).

St. Paul thrived on such "warring" terms as *battle, struggle, war, purification, control* and *mortification*. Christians were gladiators going to do battle and only those who endured to the very end would receive the crown. Pseudo-Macarius translates St. Paul's doctrine into a teaching that would be not only repeated by all the desert Fathers, but that would be the platform by which they lived their desert life:

> Whoever truly wishes to please God and truly makes himself an enemy against the adversary must wage battle on a double front. One battle takes place in the material affairs of this life by turning completely away from the earthly preoccupations and the attractions of world bonds and from the sinful passions. The other battle takes place in the interior against the evil spirits themselves of whom the apostle spoke. . . . Whenever anyone listens to the Word of God and enters into the battle and throws off all the concerns of this life and the bonds of the world and denies himself all fleshly pleasures and breaks away from these, then, as he attends to the Lord perseveringly, he is able to find in his heart another struggle, another hidden opposition and another way of the temptations of the evil spirits and another battle opens up. And thus by standing firm and calling on the Lord in unshaken faith and with great patience and expecting help to come from him, he can obtain from him inward deliverance of the evil spirits who operate in the area of the hidden passions.[1]

With Cassian, the Fathers considered the spiritual combat to be the means by which the Christian would reach spiritual perfection.[2] In the fray all virtues were to be acquired, especially love.[3] The monks deliberately sought out the most forsaken places of the desert to do the battle. Their spirit was one of aggressiveness, of rushing into the attack against the evil spirits, of precipitating the battle since eventually the battle had to set its lines inside the individual's heart.

DEVILS

Relying on what Holy Scripture says about the spiritual life as a battle or war against the evil spirits (Eph 6:12; Rv 12; Gn 2) the demonology, expressed in the *Life of Antony* written by St. Anthanasius, and in the writings of Evagrius and Cassian, becomes the classic description of the spiritual combat among the Fathers of the desert, and hence in traditional ascetical writings down through the ages. No doubt Greek philosophy and certain Judaic currents prevalent two centuries before the time of Christ had influenced the thinking of the desert writers in regard to the activities of the demons in the world.[4] But the Christian writers all agreed on one point: The demons exercised a cosmic force over the entire world and it was the duty of the desert athletes to purify the world of demons by means of faith in the power of God and through ascetical practices that would lead to the fulfillment of the Christian life and the development of Christian love toward God and the entire world.

Sinful people were not attacked by the devils, according to the Fathers' teaching for they were already in bondage. It was those who were striving for perfection who attracted the attacks of the demons, according to Origen.[5] The devils could not cause human beings to sin. Yet Evagrius admits that they can introduce phantasies and images into the human mind. It is, thus, in the mind that the most intense battle is waged.

> The demons strive against men of the world chiefly through their deeds, but in the case of monks for the most part by means of thoughts, since the desert deprives them of such affairs. Just as it is easier to sin by thought than by deed, so also is the war fought on the field of thought more severe than that which is conducted in the area of things and events. For the mind is easily moved indeed, and hard to control in the presence of sinful phantasies.[6]

The demons cleverly watch us, observe our weak points, and then attack with their phantasies.

LOGISMOI

Logismoi, which may be of good or bad nature, are images—sensible phantasms that, when dwelt upon, draw us toward an object existing outside of ourselves. They are not the same as mere thoughts, which the Greek philosophers called *noema.* The object need not to be evil in itself, but given our fallen nature and the distortion introduced into us through the effects of original sin, we are drawn to it rather than to those things suggested by our hearts under the inspiration of grace. The Fathers were concerned with the psychology of image-temptations in the area of evil *logismoi.* Such images become evil as we accept them and thus feed the cancerous growth of self-love within our heart.

There could be no true prayer or surrendering love with deep consciousness of God's otherness and our identity as children of God if there were such noisy distractions buzzing within our mind. To pray in tranquillity *(hesychia)* means to pray in total gift of self to God by being completely centered upon his loving presence. We should check each thought that might lead to a scattering of attention away from God toward self. Pseudo-Macarius describes in a simple analogy the workings of a mind amid distracting thoughts:

> The soul, being tainted by sin, is similar to a large forest on a mountain or like reeds in a river or thick, thorny bushes. Whoever pass through such a place need to hold out their hands before them and with force and labor push aside whatever lies in their path. So also the thoughts that come from the adverse power beset the soul. Therefore, there is need for great diligence and mental alertness so that one may distinguish those outside thoughts that rise by the power of the adversary.[7]

Evagrius, the master-psychologist who articulated for the desert Fathers the inner workings of the human mind as it underwent the invisible combat, describes a *logismos* not as a mere thought, but as an image, a phantasm that springs forth, not from the highest part of the mind, the spirit *(nous)* but from the cognitive faculty *(dianoia)*. It is in the discursive area of the mind that such a phantasm makes its appearance and presents itself as something attractive. Its power is to move the spirit in a "passionate" movement, a desire to possess the object for the pleasure and power that it will bring.[8]

DEVELOPMENT OF A TEMPTATION

The devils can play with these phantasms that are stored up from our sensible, perceptive life, and through them they can bring us to the first step of a temptation. Here the Fathers of the desert universally employ the stages in the development of a "passionate" temptation as given by Climacus.[9]

Climacus teaches five steps in the development of a thought temptation: the arising in our mind of a representation, a subject, an image or a phantasm; the pondering of the image in a "conversation," a turning it about in the mind, a dialogue or a discursive process of rationalizing; consenting to the thought with some pleasure; being enslaved or bound as this consent is readily given time and again; and, finally, falling so completely under the power of the suggestion that we are no longer free but are powerfully impelled to carry through at the first sight of the given phantasm (passion).

Great diligence, the Fathers exhort us, must be shown in the first moment, in the stage of presentation of the thought, before it takes over and leads us to consent. Because of our sinful nature we must be extremely attentive and never become complacent in our peaceful tranquillity of acquired virtues, for we can succumb to such temptations easily.[10]

GUARDING THE HEART

A word found repeatedly in the writings of the Fathers is *prosochi*, attention. Other words or phrases, such as *guarding of the heart, vigilance, sobriety,* and *purifying the heart* are used to express the inner state of alertness necessary to check every thought at the entryway to our consciousness. This is all summarized in the teachings of the Fathers around the doctrine of *nepsis* or sober vigilance. *Nepo* means to be sober, not inebriated or intoxicated. It means, therefore, a sort of mental sobriety, a mental balance, an internal disposition that keeps us in what Teilhard de Chardin calls, in his *Divine Milieu,* "passionate indifference." In this state we are not moved by our passions, but we hold ourselves attentive and in abeyance until we know what this or that thought is all about. Does God want me to yield to this or not? Is it going to take me away from God? If it does, out it goes in that very first moment of awareness. *Nepsis* is not only that interior awareness of the possibility of the devil coming in by these infiltrating thoughts, but it is also the whole development through vigilance of the virtuous correspondence to God's voice within us. It is living according to God's *Logos* as the Spirit reveals to us interiorly the right way of acting as children of a loving Father. It is the measurement of how integrated we have become by God's grace. The total *I* corresponds as a unity to the Word of God. Instead of passions tearing us apart or pulling us in their own directions, we find an inner harmony that grows each time we are faithful to the living Word within us.

The Fathers cite from the Book of Joshua 5:13: "Are you with us or with our enemies?" The attentive, alert Christian is to place a guard or sentinel at the door of the mind and to question each thought that seeks entrance into the consciousness.[11] Such attention requires the gift of discernment of spirits to decide what comes from evil spirits and what may be from God.

DISCERNMENT

As the Fathers' chief preoccupation centered around incessant prayer, it was imperative for them to stress the discernment of spirits in order to eradicate any forces that would take them from a conscious self-surrendering at each moment to please

God. The scriptures present us continually with symbols that in-dicate that within all of us there lies a choice between good and bad (for example Gn 2:17). A divine, mysterious voice from within our heart speaks God's word and draws us toward God while a sinister voice gently tempts us to eat the forbidden fruit. What criterion is the Christian to use to discern these two spirits? The prophets aided the Israelites to discern what God was saying to them. The sapiential literature spoke of the way of the wise man over the foolish and sinful man. St. Paul speaks of discernment of spirits as a gift of the Holy Spirit (1 Cor 12:10).[12]

For the Fathers, discernment of spirits was an important aspect of the spiritual life. The ideal was to have the help of an intelligent, Spirit-filled director or spiritual father to whom one daily revealed the content of his thoughts and his reactions to them.[13] St. Antony insists that there is need of much prayer and asceticism in order to receive the gift of discernment of spirits from the Holy Spirit and thus be able to recognize each of the evil demons disguised behind various phantasms.[14] Such discernment cannot come without a lifetime of observing how the demons operate and how one reacts to such temptations. Evagrius writes:

> Let him observe their intensity, their periods of decline and follow them as they rise and fall. Let him note well the complexi-ty of his thoughts, their periodicity, the demons which cause them, with the order of their succession and the nature of their associations. Then let him ask from Christ the explanations of these data he has observed. For the demons become thoroughly infuriated with those who practice active virtue in a manner that is increasingly contemplative.[15]

Such observation will yield gradually to a special sense, a spiritual intuition that in a flash will recognize an evil thought and the presence of the demons.[16] The experience of those athletes who have observed well the workings of the demons has been written down, starting with Origen and, above all, Evagrius.

THE EIGHT PASSIONATE THOUGHTS

The demons, as Evagrius observes, attack through the avenues of the body, soul and spirit. There are basically eight doors or passionate thoughts through which the demons seek entrance into the human consciousness. Origen gives a commentary on the Book of Deuteronomy in which he calls the seven tribes that Joshua fought the seven concupiscences or the seven capital sins. But he actually ends up with eight. The first one is found before the Israelites enter the desert; they were faced with the vice of gluttony, represented by the fleshpots of Egypt.[17]

Starting from the more sensible enticements, Evagrius moves to the more intellectual temptations. These capital temptations, the root of all other temptations and sins, are: gluttony, fornication, covetousness, anger, sadness, acedia (ennui or boredom with the struggle for perfection), vainglory and pride.[18] Acedia is unique to the Eastern Fathers' list of basic temptations and arises out of the desert monk's pursuit of perfection in solitude as a temptation to discourage his spiritual progress.

DEVELOPING THE VIRTUES

The *praxis* or ascetical life, the spiritual battle, was not merely an effort to eradicate the negative influence of the demonic forces from outside as well as from within the mind of the Christian, but its greater accent was placed on developing the Christian virtues so that there would be a constant state of "oneness" with the indwelling, risen Jesus by putting on his mind. The Fathers knew that the essence of the Christian life was to fall in love with God who has loved mankind infinitely in his son Jesus. Yet this was to be not only an affective response, one in feeling only, but it was to be an *effective* response in doing the commands laid down in God's revealed word. Thus obedience to God's holy will was an essential part of the spiritual combat that positively developed Christian love within the individual to enable him to pray always, that is, to live always consciously in God's holy presence in a "doing" surrender at each moment to please him.

One phrase that summarized for the Fathers of the desert the positive aspect of developing virtues was "to observe the commands of God." The deceits of the demons are overcome by observing faithfully the commands of God. The fulfillment of God's holy will had to be for the Fathers the sign of true love, the end of the spiritual life. Jesus had clearly taught this and the Fathers were being obedient to God's Word: "If anyone loves me he will keep my word, and my Father will love him, and we shall come to him and make our home with him. Those who do not love me do not keep my words" (Jn 14:23). God has created the human soul with three powers: the irascible, the concupiscible and the rational appetites. God, in order that these powers may enjoy full "health" and attain the end for which he created them, gives commands for each power of the soul. The devils, in order to destroy this health and take the soul away from God, attack the soul with temptations that violate the God-given commandments.

Some commands of God look only to exterior actions, such as corporal works of mercy. Other commands are more spiritual and these are more comprehensive, containing in themselves many other exterior commands of God. Thus the fulfillment of these interior commands of God insures the fulfillment also of all the exterior ones. Christ came to give us a new list of commands, the Beatitudes which are the commands of God for all. In the patristic tradition there is no separation into various spiritualities, one type for celibates, clergymen and religious, and another type for the married or single in the world.[19] All are commanded by Christ to be pure of heart and to be humble of heart. All virtues are contained in these two, which further narrow down to one all-embracing command: "Love God with your whole soul, your whole heart and all your strength."

The Fathers are less systematic in developing the area of Christian virtues than the scholastic theologians. Virtues were the measure of one's divinization by grace into the likeness of God. Origen called Jesus Christ all the virtues; he is Justice, Wisdom, Truth, etc.[20] Practice of virtues is a true participation in the nature of Christ.

CHARITY

One accent that the Fathers inherited from Plato and Aristotle is that all virtues are interconnected in a unity. Thus all the virtues must be developed equally or none of them will be effective. St. Gregory of Nyssa writes, "It is impossible that one virtue exists without the other for virtue must be perfect."[21] They unanimously agree that the virtue of charity perfectly embraces all the others. St. John Chrysostom insists that charity is the summit of the spiritual mountain of the virtues.[22] Charity among the trinity of virtues that make us godly, along with faith and hope, is the goal of all other virtues. Without charity there can be no true Christian life. St. Symeon the New Theologian writes that charity is acquired not by our efforts alone, but by the operations of the Holy Spirit within us.

> For love is not a name, but the divine essence, both participable and yet incomprehensible, but totally divine. . . . This is, therefore, why I have said that love is comprehensible and it is personalized insofar as it is communicable and understandable.[23]

Yet it is a curious fact that the Fathers rarely speak about charity in comparison with their numerous writings about the *praxis* involved in extirpating negativity from their lives. They believed that charity was a great mystery that had to be experienced from within, and would then flow out in true Christian love for others according to the circumstances of each person's life. No doubt their highly developed sense of humility and also their fear of being deluded kept them in the more practical aspect of true love, namely, the serious application of themselves to removing all obstacles that prevented them from truly loving as Christians ought.[24]

Thus the one great commandment that the Fathers insist upon is to love God completely. In doing this, they would be filled with the divinizing love of God's uncreated energies filling them with a godly love for others. The end of the spiritual life is love of God and neighbor. The *praxis* is the index of how seriously we give ourselves to the interior struggle against self-love to reach a state of "passionate passionlessness."

APATHEIA

The continued struggle to uproot the negative control that passionate temptations exert over us, and the positive putting on through our virtuous living of the mind of Christ, measure perfection by the state of integration that the Fathers call *apatheia*. This concept has been greatly misunderstood by Westerners since it has been taken from a Stoic philosophy that would imply either stoic apathy or at least the deadening of our passions. The Stoics tried to cut out of existence the four predominant passions of joy, pain, desire for a future good, and sorrow at an impending future evil. Christians made the important distinction that none of these passions were evil in themselves. One could not take the first step in sanctity if he or she did not have the desire to love God and a certain fear of sin.

The state that the Eastern Fathers sought as the goal of all *praxis*, called *apatheia*, is a state of self-control. We allow the grace of God to filter down into our hearts and be the sole determinant of our actions. We no longer act without reflection. True love has conquered the heart and we wait gently to see what line of action or thought would be most "loving" toward God who has so completely loved us into being. Only those who have control of all inordinate passions can act constantly in such a virtuous manner by living totally under the virtue of Jesus Christ.

This is where *praxis* and inner stillness of all thoughts in prayer meet in the gift of mystical contemplation or *theoria*. The sign of a new infusion of mystical illumination obtained through purity of heart and the gift of tears is the stilling of all passionate thoughts that tend to direct us toward sin. Through *apatheia* we enter into a reintegration of our whole being: senses, emotion, intellect and will. We become rooted in God in tranquillity, a peaceful resting that is very dynamic in its seeking always the good pleasure of God, far removed from any self-centered quietism.

G. Bardy, the famous patrologist, describes *apatheia* as found in the writings of the Greek Fathers:

> It is not a matter of insensibility towards God whom one must love above all else, nor of insensibility towards men, but of perfect liberty of spirit, perfect abandonment as the fruit of renunciation, perfect detachment from all things, humility, continual mortification and contempt for the body. This is a very lofty doctrine in which *apatheia* is brought back to human proportions . . . and no longer has any of the rigorousness which the Stoics assigned to it.[25]

There is nothing of the Stoic "apathy" or noninvolving indifference toward others and the world around us. *Apatheia* is totally dependent on God's grace, a state impossible for us to attain by our own powers. The Fathers of the desert described it as the state in which the mind is motionless in the heart. This gift has its beginning in prayer and is first bestowed during prayer. It is the return to Eden and the restoration of man and woman in Christ, the fulfillment of God's plan to make man and woman according to the image and likeness of God that is Jesus Christ. It is entering into the true freedom of sons and daughters of a loving Father. It is sharing in the fullness of life that Jesus came to bring us (Jn 10:10).

St. Isaac the Syrian summarizes what *apatheia* meant to the athletes of the desert:

> When the soul undergoes such spiritual activity and subjects itself completely to God and through direct union nears the

divinity and is enlightened in its movements by an interior light from above and the mind experiences a feeling of future happiness, then it forgets itself, its temporal existence on this earth, and loses any attraction for the things of this earth; there is enkindled in it an ineffable joy, an indescribable sweetness warms the heart, the whole body feels its repercussions and man forgets not only his plaguing passions, but also even life itself and thinks that the kingdom of heaven consists of nothing other than this blissful condition. Here in this state he experiences that love of God is sweeter than life and intelligence, now in accordance with God's will from which springs love, is sweeter than honey and the honeycomb.[26]

REINTEGRATION

Evagrius and the other writers of desert spirituality are using the model common in all "immanent" religions that describes integration as the movement of a person from outward dispersion (a disposition to possess objects in order to feed self-love) to a harmonious oneness, an inner stillness of all one's faculties.

Apatheia, therefore, does not mean to atrophy any part of a human being's makeup, but, rather, it refers to the total reintegration of a person brought into the freedom of loving submission at all times to God's will. Dispersion through self-love is slavery. *Apatheia* is true freedom through pure love of God and neighbor. It is liberation from all elements in our lives that impede us from loving and worshipping God. It frees us from *eros* or self-centered love to love with God's love, *agape*, directing us at every moment.

It does not imply impeccability or the impossibility of ever sinning, nor does it mean one will never again be tempted. It means, and this admits of great growth, that the depths of one's being are fully committed to the love of God and, therefore, one would now have to wrench himself or herself in great interior violence in order to sin. *Apatheia* is not the end. It still demands to be perfected in ongoing contemplation and true loving of God and neighbor.

PASSIONS

Apatheia has as its end the extirpation of human *passion*. It is precisely in this area that a balanced interpretation is needed. Western theologians, following St. Thomas, distinguish between passions in the metaphysical sense and passions in the psychological sense. Passion in the metaphysical sense refers to the state of a person receiving some action from outside forces. Passion in the psychological sense refers to the God-given sensitive appetites within us, the concupiscible and irascible passions.[27] If we read the desert Fathers with the latter meaning of passion, then we can see only a very distorted, dehumanizing Christianity. Then it would seem that passions are neither good nor indifferent; that instead they are "sicknesses" of the human soul.[28] We would assume that the passions are not part of our metaphysical makeup; that they were not present until the fall of the first man.

Although the Fathers do not have a fixed, scientific description or definition for passions, they are all agreed that they refer to a natural, necessary instinct that God has given to aid us human beings to live "according to the image and likeness" of God. However, through sin, they have become an excessive, irrational, immoderate instinct that is no longer submissive to reason or God's Logos.[29] St. Gregory of Nyssa describes passions as powers created by God. Sin, however, introduced into human nature a foreign element from outside of man's basically good nature. Now the passions become dangerous because the highest spiritual faculties in man can no longer direct them.

For St. Gregory of Nyssa, man, after sin, is no longer the perfect, full image of God. To express this view of man as immersed in matter and tending toward self-centeredness rather than toward loving submission to God, he uses the image of the garment of skins that now clothes each man and woman. This is a state of corruptibility that means more than that man is destined to die a physical death and his body will become eventually corrupt. This is a state that describes man's orientation away from God, the loss of God's divine life within man. Yet this state of passion in which fallen humanity finds itself is precisely the "locus" or situation in which it is to meet the healing savior. Jesus enters into that state of corruptibility or state of passion in order to lead us into the life of incorruptibility or life eternal.[30]

St. Maximus the Confessor describes *philautia*, self-love or bias toward self, as the root of all passions.[31] At the root of all sin is a movement toward exaltation of self over God or others.

TRANSFORMATION OF PASSIONS

What we should take from the Fathers' teachings about the passions is that whatever the degree of involvement in passionate attachments, be they on a bodily, psychical or spiritual plane, there is no state of alienation that cannot be brought back into reconciliation with the heavenly Father by Jesus Christ and his Spirit of love. There is no state of inner "sickness," of the death of God's life in us through an excessive bias toward self, that cannot be healed by Christ meeting us in our brokenness. He has become a part of this disoriented world. He, too, was tempted toward "passion" and the world of "corruptibility." But he resisted by self-discipline and love for the Father and for ourselves. St. Maximus the Confessor gives the final word on the subject of passion and the whole aim of the spiritual combat. All passion is able to be healed "through abstinence and charity."[32]

INTERPRETATION

Perhaps in no area of the Fathers' spiritual writings do we find more difficulty, confusion and even repugnance to the doctrine proposed than in the matter of asceticism. And yet, perhaps, it is precisely what the early Fathers have taught us from their own experience as ascetics and mystics concerning the interior battle over the forces of evil and the conquest of Christ in our hearts that we today most need. We need to demythologize the images and symbols that the writers of the Old and New Testaments and the Fathers of the desert used to describe the spiritual battle.

Today we do not feel comfortable with talk about demons or devils attacking us (unless we belong to evangelical churches that, like the Fathers, use the symbol language of the Bible). We suspect persons who are so introspective that day and night they are checking their "spiritual temperature." The heroic (and even at times bizarre) ascetical practices of the desert athletes not only no longer edify us, but even cause us to wonder at their understanding of what true Christianity is all about.

Amid all their symbols and exploits there is something that fascinates us about the writings of such early Christians. They, in a word, were *fiercely* bent on seeking to love God with their whole "heart." This meant for them an *effective* desire to eradicate from their lives anything that would compromise or hinder their growth in fulfilling the great commands of God: to love God and neighbor with all their strength. Their heroic, constant dedication shouts out to us that nothing, not even their own lives, was ultimate—only God was.

They rightly saw the Christian life as a struggle. Jesus called it a *cross*, a denial of our very own lives in order to find our true life in him. After all the demythologizing is done on what the Fathers (or the writers of the Gospel) meant in their writings, there still remains the terrifying truth that sums up the *raison d'être* of their desert lives. They knew there were inimical forces, not only around them in the "world," but, above all, within them. These forces had to *die*, but only in order that Jesus Christ might live as complete Lord in their lives.

THE DEVIL REVISITED

Theologians today are examining the traditional teaching on devils as presented in Holy Scripture and in ordinary piety. We have seen how Evagrius and all of the other desert Fathers wrote about a world of objectified demons or devils, much in the fashion of the biblical writers.

In the Gospels we find Jesus meeting persons who were possessed by the devil or by many devils. In Mt 17:15 Jesus heals a boy tormented by a demon. The epileptic boy was healed when the demon left him. Those possessed by devils in the Gospels were not always sinful persons held in bondage by some physical or psychical sickness. A clear distinction such as we would make today between being ill (especially mentally) and being possessed by a devil is not found.

The Fathers speak of the devils as fallen spirits that attack us from outside and can influence our phantasms. These forces can entice us through temptations or attractive images planted in our imagination. When dwelled upon by us, these can stir our higher deliberative powers to choose such objects, and eventually sin through choosing self-love over love of God and neighbor. What should we hold from such descriptions? The desert Fathers literally went into the desert just as Jesus is reported in the Gospel accounts to have done. He was tempted three times by the devil. Is this an exact report or a literary genre to describe something very real and very historical but an experience that cannot be gotten at unless the writers use mythopoetic language?

The essential teachings of the Fathers of the desert do not depend on whether they literally encountered a fallen angel, the devil. They were describing in the symbols of the spiritual world an adversary, an opposing force that was exercising a very negative power over them. The Israelites were tempted in the desert and succumbed. The first man and woman in Eden yielded to this tempting force. Jesus also encountered such a force in the desert and all through his life (Heb 4:15), but he resisted.

The Fathers give us from their own experiences a strategy for resisting the forces that attack from without and from within our very own minds.

The demons stand for all powers that oppose the work of God and his "ministering spirits" (Heb 1:14) to divinize us into children of God. These are very real powers operating with wickedness and cunning. And yet these forces cannot be pinpointed to only concrete agents. They stand for all enemies to our growth as loving human beings. It is a mystery whether God truly works through spirits to govern the universe. It will always remain a mystery whether fallen angelic spirits roam about the universe, as St. Paul and the Fathers of the desert seemingly held.

The brokenness in a world that is filled with selfishness is still around us. Such "unnaturalness," that is, a state of nature not being what it should be, touches us through individual persons living today. We are gripped by attacking evils through our own sinfulness from our past actions and from the actions of persons who left their marks on our unconscious through memories. Such memories, through phantasms, can stir up new relationships, new callings toward further selfishness.

Jesuit Father Juan B. Cortes, professor of psychology at Georgetown University, believes *demon* is used for what we call today a "complex" or an "emotional" conflict.[33] C.G. Jung and other psychologists have indicated the power of the unconscious to store up and even evolve experiences that are hidden from the normal flow of consciousness. St. Paul described the spiritual enemies, the devils, as enemies warring outside of us, "For it is not against human enemies that we have to struggle, but against the Sovereignties and the Powers who originate the darkness in this world, the spiritual army of evil in the heavens" (Eph 6:12). He also gives a psychological description of a human being "attacked" by a principle of evil and sin that seemingly is lodged inside his body: "my body follows a different law that battles against the law which my reason dictates.

This is what makes me a prisoner of that law of sin which lives inside my body'' (Rom 7:23).

Presence of the demonic within us cannot be reached by reasoning. It can only be accepted by those who experience what St. Paul, the other writers of Holy Scripture and the patristic and mystic writers down through the centuries have experienced. These writers used mythic language to describe a common experience, yet one open only to those who live interiorly. For those who have had similar experiences, the mythic language can never be anything but a carrier to describe a reality that goes far beyond a scientific, observable-by-the-senses description. Such a reality is so present and embraces so many factors from an individual's life that only mythopoetic language can be used. Thus the language of demons speaks of a very present reality, but only to those who live interiorly as the Fathers of the desert lived.

INNER ALERTNESS

The psychology of the hesychastic Fathers concerning the development of a thought-temptation is not, however, expressed in a myth. Their language is nuanced and comes out of very real experiences that happened to them day and night. We can relate to these experiences. We can see how our bodily appetites are constantly drawing us to excess. We want to eat the most delicious foods, drink the best wines, enjoy sexual pleasures and delight in the eyes and the other senses. Unless we are careful such appetites will carry us to immoderation and excess.

The eight categories of basic temptations proposed by the Fathers were not meant to be a definitive listing to replace the Decalogue. They represent concrete areas that cut across a human being's existence in body, soul and spirit relationships. The five stages by which a temptation unfolds and the emphasis on an inner attentiveness to catch the first appearance of such a *logismos,* a mental phantasm, and bring it under the scrutiny of the Gospel values are still valuable spiritual teaching for us.

APPLICATION

We have seen the teaching of the hesychastic Fathers of the desert in viewing the Christian life as a spiritual combat. We have seen how they used very often mythopoetic language similar to that of the writers of the Old and New Testaments to describe a pressing reality that can be experienced by all human beings throughout all ages, namely, that there is a world of negativity. This world operates within us and outside of us with a powerful aggressiveness that we can combat successfully only with a similar aggressiveness on our part added to God's grace. We have sought, therefore, to sift through such imagery and to arrive at an interpretation that would give us the wheat grains that could bring us true spiritual nourishment. How can we apply to ourselves in the 20th century the Fathers' extensive teachings on the "battle" aspect of the Christian life?

We can be exhorted, not only from scripture, but from the Fathers who interpreted scripture and lived out the essential teaching of scripture in their ascetical and mystical lives, that we have need constantly and throughout our whole life for vigilance against the sinful elements around and within us. It is not a mere waiting but an exercise of faith in God's power within us to come to our rescue and help us in the battle.

> Be calm but vigilant, because your enemy the devil is prowling round like a roaring lion, looking for someone to eat. Stand up to him, strong in faith (1 Pt 5:8-9).

We are to observe the inner movements of our thoughts which tend through our sinful involvement in what St. Paul defined as the "sarx" or "flesh" situation toward self-centeredness. Thus an attentive heart is always needed to catch any movements toward selfishness in our thoughts before they become actuated in our deeds.

Positively, we need to be vigilant over our thoughts in order to put on the mind of Jesus Christ. This embraces the whole area of developing Christian virtues, which is nothing other than always acting out of love of God and neighbor. To love God effectively we must follow the advice of St. Paul:

> Every thought is our prisoner, captured to be brought into obedience to Christ. Once you have given your complete obedience, we are prepared to punish any disobedience (2 Cor 10:5-6).

SELF-REFLECTION

Knowledge of our "existential" self, that is, the person we are at any given moment in need of specific areas of healing, can be had only if we take time out each day to reflect upon our thoughts, words and actions according to the normative values of the Gospel and God's personal "graceful" interaction with us at each moment. This means a turning within to examine our motivation and value system at work in every thought, word and deed. This is not an easy task and demands daily attention since through years of life-experiences our "false" self has built up defense mechanisms that insulate us from our true self that lies deeply embedded within our unconscious. Such defenses seem to protect us from the threatening forces around us. Yet they also prevent us from becoming more self-directing, from overcoming past conditionings and painful experiences that negatively affect our relationships with God, the world and other human beings.

The Fathers have always insisted upon the daily examination of conscience as a preparation to "confessing" such thoughts, words and actions to the spiritual father. John Climacus gives the example of several monks who carried small notebooks on their persons and wrote down their thoughts each day to show their director.[34] This is meant, in our own application, to be more than mere analytical reflection. We are to be transcendently self-present to God as our Divine Physician. Such an exercise, when made each day in a prayerful encounter with God under the guidance of his Spirit of love, can be a most important part of our spiritual combat. Without it there will be little advance in deeper prayer and Christian perfection. I have outlined such an exercise of five steps in a small work entitled *Reflective Healing*.[35]

THE CROSS

Through vigilant attention to the interior movements of our heart, we will soon see what the hesychastic Fathers insisted upon, that the great enemy, preventing us from responding generously to God's call to share his divine life, is *ourselves* in our self-love or self-centeredness. We do have the "old man" within all of us (Col 3:9; Eph 4:22). There must be an all-out war to exterminate our self-love (1 Cor 10:6-11). This is the daily cross that the soldier of Christ is bidden to carry. Jesus set us an example of such successful fighting. "Christ did not think of himself" (Rom 15:3). More positively, he sought always to please his Father (Jn 8:29).

Thus self-abnegation, both negative and positive, is absolutely necessary in our lives. There must be a checking, inhibiting, nullifying of the inclinations that gravitate toward self as the center of all of our desires. We need to replace this with God as the center of all our aspirations. Instead of concentrating most of our spiritual efforts on the negative aspects and on legalism, we need to radically transform the springs of our daily activities through a movement that comes out of a deep interiority. This keeps us in touch with the indwelling Trinity, living within and guiding us according to our ultimate end.

Authentic Christian holiness consists in the flexibility to always move toward God. Asceticism reflecting a faith that embraces the cross of self-denial becomes an act of obedience to the Father, cost what it may to the individual Christian. Asceticism for modern Christians, not living in the desert, but in cities, must primarily consist in a gentle spirit that listens attentively to God's Spirit revealing God's infinite love at each moment in each event. It is in such moments that God is experienced as love, and we are loved into new being as loving children of a loving Father, brothers and sisters to one another in that same love.

INDIVIDUAL VIGILANCE

No one can describe in detail, beyond the principles as the Fathers have given them to us, how we should uproot sinfulness in our lives. The context of daily life varies from person to person. The endowments and needs of our bodies, souls and spirits are different. We, more than the secluded desert Fathers, are to seek in our daily work, in our social apostolate to make this a more humane world in which to live. We are to use the pleasures and beauties of nature, art and science, to use food, drink and television in proper moderation so that they become helps by which we can better love and serve God and neighbor.

VICTORY

The Fathers constantly lead us to the blazing furnace, similar to that into which Azariah and his companions were thrown by King Nebuchadnezzar (Dn 3:24-50). When we have the courage to turn within and enter into the spiritual battle that so often resembles the flames of that furnace, we will discover also, as did the desert athletes, that the indwelling Trinity comes to us as an "angel," fanning the flames of fire away and bring an inner coolness, as from wind and dew.

We will continuously experience new birth as children of God. As we recognize our interior brokenness in our creaturely poverty and become purified of all inordinate attachments to self by living the virtues of the Gospel, we will experience true contemplation of God as love. No longer is he outside or an object to us. We enter progressively more and more into the most intimate union with the trinitarian community that gives us our true identity as persons loved uniquely by a Father, Son and Spirit. The spiritual life is a combat, yes, but it leads to certain victory!

6.

THE JESUS PRAYER

One of the great joys of my life as a priest has been to travel about the United States and Canada and meet so many Christians on fire with the love of God and neighbor. Meeting such people, I feel as though I am reading a modern version of the *Acts of the Apostles.* People similar to Stephen, Cornelius, Lydia and Dorcas are living as disciples of Jesus Christ in the Bronx, Toronto, San Francisco and Des Moines. The Spirit is truly breathing all over this land!

Above all, such people are God's desert people, crying out in their existential inner poverty for a deeper, more prayerful relationship with Jesus Christ. The hunger for deeper prayer was not always present in American Christianity, but I pray that the present phenomenon is here to stay and will expand in new and exciting ways.

For many Christians the search has led to the discovery of the Jesus Prayer. They have found in Eastern Christian spirituality a form of prayer that transcends the discursive method they have used since childhood. This is a "meta-rational" prayer of the heart that grew out of the Jesus event experienced by the first Christian community in Jerusalem under the power of the Holy Spirit.

The early Christians of the East came to know that Jesus was more than a doctrine. He was true Life that lived within them, releasing his Spirit and divinizing them ever more into living members of his own body, the church. They knew and experienced the power of the name of Jesus as a presence operating within the context of their daily lives. They knew by faith and experience that there was simply no other name by which they would be healed and saved (Acts 4:12). Because Jesus Christ obeyed the Father in imaging his infinite love for us by emptying himself on the cross, the Father gave him the name that is above all other names, the name before which every knee should bend in adoration (Phil 2:9-11).

THE JESUS PEOPLE

When Constantine accepted Christianity as the official religion of the Roman Empire, Christians were no longer persecuted and martyred for the sake of Jesus Christ. In the fourth century the Spirit of Jesus drove thousands of men and women into the deserts of Egypt and Syria. There, as we have seen in the earlier chapters, they strove to live constantly in the consciousness of God's loving presence and to surrender themselves completely to his holy will.

From earliest times in Christianity people sought an expanded consciousness of God's abiding presence living within them. They reached out for an ever-increasing awareness, constancy and sincerity in their relationship with God. The hermits who fled into the stark, barren deserts of the East were seeking an expansion of consciousness that God was truly God in their lives. They were seeking, under the guidance of the Holy Spirit, to love God with their whole heart, their whole mind and their whole strength.

Out of the desert hesychastic spirituality grew the Jesus Prayer, a technical term of Byzantine spirituality which designates the invocation of the name of Jesus, either alone or inserted into the more or less classical formula, "Lord, Jesus Christ, Son of God, have mercy upon me a sinner."[1] That such a simple cry of the name of Jesus or the formula that gradually became accepted as the Jesus Prayer grew to epitomize Byzantine hesychastic spirituality or the prayer of the heart has to be explained by looking into the roots of both the Old and New Testaments.

THE POWER OF THE NAME OF JESUS

The Jews of the Old Testament had a special reverence for the name of God. God's name was seen as an extension of his person, as a revelation of his being and an expression of his power.[2] The name pronounced reverently by a person or invoked upon a country brought one into the very presence of God. New and intimate relationships exist between God and that people or person (Gn 48:16; Dt 28:10; Am 9:12). The name abides in the temple because God is present there personally (1 Kgs 8:10-13). In the Psalms, the divine name is called upon as a refuge, an auxiliary power, an object to be loved and worshipped.[3]

The New Testament gives us a fuller theology of God's name and the power that emanates from the reverent pronouncing of the name of Jesus. St. Paul exhorts the Philippians to call upon the name of Jesus (Phil 2:9-10). "There is no other name under heaven given to men whereby we must be saved," writes St. Peter (Acts 4:12). In St. John's Gospel Jesus reveals the power of his name to his disciples: "Hitherto, you have not asked anything in my name. . . . If you ask the Father anything in my name, he will give it to you" (Jn 16:23-24).

Basically the hesychastic Fathers saw such a short formula, repeated often day and night and even synchronized with their breathing, as a way to fulfill the scriptural exhortations to pray always (1 Thes 5:17; Eph 6:18; Lk 18:1; Lk 21:36). Meditating on the Good News of the New Testament, these early Christians accepted Jesus as the Son of God. They preached in his name and performed miracles and healings in that name. They encountered him in the sacraments which were administered in his sacred name.

There was no tone of magic; only a deep conviction that Jesus Christ, true God and true man, who died and was raised up by his heavenly Father, still lived within them and was leading them to a share in his resurrected life. Thus they cried out his name as Lord. But they also realized at every moment that they were in need of his healing mercy because of their own sinfulness. The cry of the blind man on the road to Jericho became their cry, "Lord, Jesus Christ, son of David, have pity on me a sinner" (Lk 18:38). The humble prayer of the publican in the back of the synagogue became their own, "O God, be merciful to me a sinner" (Lk 18:13). The oft-repeated *Kyrie eleison* ("Lord have mercy") of the Christian liturgies became their plea.

Through the writings of Pseudo-Macarius, Diadochus of Photike, John Climacus, Hesychius of Mount Sinai and Pseudo-Chrysostom, a broad spectrum of "monological" or one-word ejaculations were presented as a way of fixing one's attention upon the remembrance of the indwelling Christ. There was not yet a fixed formula; the monk was allowed to choose his "word." After Byzantine monasteries had been ravaged by invading Turkish troops, a renaissance of the Jesus Prayer developed on Mount Athos in the 13th and 14th centuries following the writings of Nicephoros and St. Gregory of Sinai. It was at this period of Byzantine spirituality that the Jesus Prayer became fixed with the formula, "Lord, Jesus Christ, Son of God, have mercy on me, a sinner," and techniques of how to synchronize this prayer with one's breathing, and how to sit, and so forth, became specified.

The temptation to mechanize such a form of prayer into a method can be attributed to a treatise called: *The Method of Hesychastic Prayer,* attributed to Nicephoros.[4] In this work we see an influence from Muslim mysticism on Byzantine spirituality and ultimately an influence from the spirituality of the Far East, especially from Hindu Yoga and Zen Buddism. Exact instructions are given on how to sit correctly and how to suppress one's breathing while gazing on one's navel. All these techniques were to help the monk concentrate on entering into the so-called "heart" or core of his being.

St. Gregory of Sinai gives in his *Instructions to Hesychasts* exact instructions on how to say the prayer:

Some of the fathers taught that the prayer should be said in full:

"Lord, Jesus Christ, Son of God, have mercy upon me." Others advised saying half, thus: "Jesus, Son of God, have mercy upon me," or "Lord Jesus Christ, have mercy upon me." or to alternate, sometimes saying it full and sometimes in a shorter form. Yet it is not advisable to pander to laziness by changing the words of the prayer too often, but to persist a certain time as a test of patience. Again, some teach the saying of the prayer with the lips; others with and in the mind. In my opinion both are advisable. For at times the mind, left to itself, becomes wearied and too exhausted to say the prayer mentally; at other times the lips get tired of this work. Therefore both methods of prayer should be used—with the lips and with the mind. But one should appeal to the Lord quietly and without agitation, so that the voice does not disturb the attention of the mind and does not thus break off the prayer, until the mind is accustomed to this doing and, receiving force from the Spirit, firmly prays within on its own.[5]

In the 18th century a renaissance again took place on Mount Athos with the publication in Greek of the *Philokalia,* a collection made by Metropolitan Macarius of Corinth (1731-1805) and Nicodemus the Hagiorite (c. 1748-1809) of writings of the hesychastic Fathers, especially those who wrote about the Jesus Prayer.[6] One result of this publication was to move the practice of the Jesus Prayer out of the protected precincts of monasteries and to give it to any lay person who could read Greek. With the translation into Slavonic of the *Philokalia* under the title, *Dobrotolubie* ("Love of the Good") by Paissy Velitchkovsky (1722-1794), the literature of the hesychastic Fathers and their teaching on the Jesus Prayer was made available to the entire Slavic world.[7] Theophan the Recluse (1815-1894) translated the *Dobrotolubie* into Russian and expanded the contents. It is mainly this translation that has made the Jesus Prayer an important element in Russian spirituality.

A great impetus to introduce the laity to the Jesus Prayer, its techniques and powerful psychosomatic effects came in the anonymous work, probably written between 1855 and 1861, entitled *The Way of a Pilgrim*.[8] When this work was translated into modern European languages after Russian emigrants brought it to the West, Western Christians began to learn of the Jesus Prayer and to practice it.[9]

INTERPRETATION

We must keep clearly in mind that the prayer of the heart is not completely synonymous with the Jesus Prayer. The first, as has already been pointed out, is much more extensive. But it can legitimately be claimed that the practice of the Jesus Prayer in Byzantine spirituality forms a vital part of hesychastic prayer and has always been thought to be its synopsis in verbal form. Its origin sprang out of the desert Fathers' desire to pray always and in the most intense, personal manner possible. They sought to encounter God through Jesus Christ and his indwelling Spirit in an interior movement that they described as the *heart*.

Thus we find in the Jesus Prayer, as in any true, Christian, prayerful encounter, an accent on the awesomeness and complete transcendence of Jesus Christ. He is Lord. He is the Creator and Redeemer of us all. He is more than just a good man, even more than a superstar. He is God! We must first recognize this terrifying fact: "Lord, Jesus Christ, Son of God!"

In authentic Christian prayer we must also recognize that we are sinners who need to cry out for God's merciful forgiveness and healing. St. James tells us to humble ourselves before God by realizing our sinfulness:

> Realize that you have been disloyal and get your hearts made true once more. As you come close to God you should be deeply sorry, you should be grieved, you should even be in tears—you will have to feel very small in the sight of God before he will set you on your feet once more (Jas 4:7-10).

When we have lost a sense of our sinfulness, we have also lost the sense of our constant need for the Giver of life to come and heal us still more. Though Jesus is our personal savior, and has saved us, we still need his healing power. "Lord Jesus Christ, have mercy on me, a sinner."

The third element that the Jesus Prayer highlights in a condensed prayer form is what binds us sinners to Jesus, the Lord and God Almighty. This is our hunger for his presence with us and within us. "More intimately to me than I to myself," wrote St. Augustine. St. Paul preached, "He is not far from any one of us. Indeed, it is in him that we live and move and have our being" (Acts 17:28). Because Jesus Christ is Lord and God, completely perfect and transcendent to all creatures, he is able also to be the ground of our being, living within us, sustaining us in being. "Through him all things came to be, not one thing had its being but through him" (Jn 1:3).

PSYCHOSOMATIC AIDS TO PRAYER

How can we interpret the use of breathing and other somatic techniques to aid prayer as taught in the practice of the Jesus Prayer? No doubt there can be great abuses and dangers when one uses psychosomatic techniques to reach new levels of consciousness. This is demonstrated not only in the history of hesychastic spirituality but in that of all spiritualities down through the ages, both Christian and non-Christian.

Yet great damage to our Christian faith can also result when we Christians ignore our bodies and other material aids in prayer and worship. One lesson that we can learn from Eastern Christian spirituality, especially from *hesychasm,* is that material techniques such as incense, icons, darkness and light, bodily prostrations and rhythmic breathing synchronized with chant or mental repetition of a Christian-type *mantra* or ejaculation can help us become integrated and centered more deeply upon the presence of the loving Trinity. We must distinguish between our physical and mental practices and God's grace in prayer, but we must not separate them from the function of liturgical or worshipping signs.

Our bodily or psychical activities function primarily as means to remove any obstacles to grace on our part. The efficacy of any of these activities, such as the techniques that grew up around the practice of the Jesus Prayer, must be judged by how well they help to bring us into the mysterious presence of God in prayer. They shall be known by their fruits, greater union with God and neighbor in our increased love and humble service shown to all.

The various techniques of breathing, sitting, fasting and repetition of the name of Jesus can be aids to center us and calm our distracted minds and hearts so that we can pray with greater concentration and consciousness.[10] Any bodily or psychical technique must be seen as a help to praying with greater consciousness, beyond our habitual, superficial level of controlled, discursive prayer. We must ask ourselves: What are we striving to do by such techniques? Will grace be "produced" automatically by the mere positing of such technical practices? Will God routinely have to bestow upon us his graces if we comply exactly with the approved techniques? We can see why the hesychastic Fathers insisted always on the intense ascetical life as part of the preparation for being open to the grace of God in prayer. Without a vigorous interior discipline psychosomatic techniques tend to become ends in themselves and the altered state of consciousness a goal in itself.

The interrelation of body, soul and spirit is becoming more evident through studies done in biofeedback and the use of such machines as electroencephalographs.

Dr. Herbert Benson, a member of the Harvard faculty of medicine, has studied the "relaxation response," the dramatic changes in heart rate, blood pressure, metabolism, and skin resistance that take place in people using the techniques basic to Transcendental Meditation (TM) and other forms of concentrated meditation such as the Jesus Prayer, that use a mantra and synchronize it with the breathing.[11]

The efficacy of any such techniques depends not on how "high" one gets, but rather on the intensity of faith, hope and

love that comes to us when in earnestness we cry out to the Holy
Spirit to infuse our hearts with these virtues in order that we
may know Jesus Christ and experience even now within our lives
the power of his resurrection and the desire to suffer with him
(Phil 3:10). The Jesus Prayer, as the Fathers taught, can never be
a mere "gimmick" or technique that attains an effect without
an interior surrendering to the love of God. It can, however, be
a most efficacious way of centering ourselves through the recall
of the name of Jesus. It is part of both the ascetical life and the
life of unceasing prayer, leading to contemplation.

DEGREES OF PRAYING THE JESUS PRAYER

The use of the Jesus Prayer will develop in various stages.
The Fathers have always taught that the prayer is first prayed
aloud by the voice or formed by the lips. This develops a
psychosomatic habit; the prayer comes easily to the mind. In the
second stage, the prayer becomes more inward. It acquires a
rhythm of its own and the mind repeats it without any conscious
act of will. In the third stage, the Jesus Prayer enters the heart,
dominating the entire personality. Its rhythm identifies with the
movement of the heart and becomes unceasing.

The use of the Jesus Prayer is a means that, with God's
grace and our continued cooperation, leads to incessant prayer.
For the Fathers this inner prayer means standing with the mind
in the heart before God, either simply living in his presence or
expressing petitions, thanksgiving or praise. Ultimately it is an
inner poverty of spirit through increased faith, hope and love,
gifts of the Holy Spirit, that allow us to be in communion with
God without any other medium. The phrase, either the traditional Jesus Prayer, or the simple one chosen by the individual,
becomes no longer a medium to usher us into the presence of
Jesus Christ but the phrase becomes one with the person of
Jesus, dwelling within the heart. St. Theophan the Recluse gives
the accepted teaching of the hesychastic Fathers:

We must acquire the habit of always being in communion with God, without any image, any process of reasoning, any perceptible movement of thought. Such is the true expression of prayer. The essence of inner prayer, or standing before God with the mind in the heart, consists precisely in this.[12]

The final perfection of the Jesus Prayer is the prayer of the heart. This takes the form of mystical prayer since the contemplative is no longer striving to pray, but the prayer exists and acts on its own because the Spirit of God prays in him or her. Prayer is no longer a series of acts but a state which fulfills St. Paul's command to pray unceasingly (1 Thes 5:17). This prayer continues within such a person, regardless of what he or she is doing—talking, writing, eating, even sleeping or dreaming.[13]

INCREASED CONSCIOUSNESS

Contemplation is, therefore, not a question of merely following a magic formula. It is a gift from God received only when a person is prepared through purification of the "heart." Nor is the contemplative stage attained when one feels an inner warmth or receives a physical perception of a divine light. (This will be treated in the following chapter.) Daily life must be the test of the efficacy of true Christian contemplation. The use of the Jesus Prayer is a way of understanding the Incarnation as a special act to bring our inner consciousness in touch with God. This is accomplished by giving us the opportunity to confront God himself in a devotion that brings about the realization of his presence as indwelling in our heart through the invocation of the name and experience of the presence of Jesus.

In this simple prayer we strive to expand our conscious awareness of God through Christ, as God reveals his presence as indwelling within us on various levels of our consciousness. As we continue to grow in consciousness of ourselves in relationship to the trinitarian Persons, Father, Son and Spirit, God continues to come alive to us throughout all of his creation. By such incessant prayer we strive to go beyond ourselves and to become united in him and in all creation. We want greater union with God because we know through experience that human life can be lived only to the fullest degree through the consciously felt presence of God in all things.

Through the increased consciousness of God in creation, we cease to suffer estrangement from the world around us. We experience ourselves in an evolving dynamism in a cosmic setting. We transcend ourselves and our own limitations only to recognize our dynamic relationship to God in all things evolving in him and through our creative work.

Relationship to fellow human beings increases. And it is then, only, that true charity, unhampered by selfishness, can begin to exist. We are no longer shackled by the merely "profane" but discover the "insideness" of all things as we discover the presence and the loving activities of God in all creatures.

APPLICATION

A busy, modern person might ask whether this type of prayer form, centered around the constant repetition of the name of Jesus or the traditional formula, has any meaning today. It is true that our lifestyle differs radically from that of the hesychastic desert Fathers who not only wrote about the Jesus Prayer but practiced it in the context of their very withdrawn lives, away from noise and multiplicity.

Still, most of us modern Christians are being drawn to a more biblically oriented prayer life. We hunger for an immediacy with the same Jesus who preached, healed and gave his divine life to a world that was sick and caught up in the darkness of self-centeredness. The security that we had once experienced within the confines of a highly structured, rationalistic theology and fixed, uniform liturgical rituals is giving way to a burning thirst on our part to experience more interiorly and more deeply the indwelling Trinity. We hunger to rediscover the beauty and the power of the name of Jesus so as to live constantly in his loving presence.

And so we ask ourselves: Can we still encounter the living Jesus Christ as Savior in our noisy, dirty, bustling cities? Can the reverent pronouncing of the sacred name of Jesus, preceded by self-purification and our dying to all inordinate self-love, bring him alive in our hearts and on our streets, at our work and in our families? If we joined this prayer to a humble plea for the ability to see the allness of God in all things as we walk about our busy cities, drive along our highways or occupy ourselves in an almost endless round of busy activities, would it not develop within us an atmosphere of God's presence that would enable us to see him shining diaphanously in all his material creation?

By seeking each day to push ourselves to greater levels of consciousness that Jesus lives within us through the repetition of his sacred name, we would gradually begin to experience him no longer as an object in heaven, in the Eucharist, or existing outside of us. We would become aware of our true selves, children of God, begotten in Jesus through his Spirit of love. We would come gradually to experience God as the core of our very being. Jesus, then, is no longer a mere concept, but a living Person, dynamically acting within us throughout our entire life. He will "com-penetrate" us so that gradually we can begin to understand the depths of union that St. Paul experienced in being one with Jesus when he wrote: ". . . I live now not with my own life but with the life of Christ who lives in me" (Gal 2:20).

DEGREES OF JESUS-PRESENCE [14]

There are various degrees of faith-appreciation of the presence of Jesus Christ in our lives. As we grow through life's desert experience into a deeper faith, our pronouncing of his holy Name will have ever greater effects on our prayer. At the beginning of our prayer life, it can be used as an ejaculation throughout the day. It can also serve as a preparation for prayer in order to integrate us, to pull us together and reach that "still point" deep within where we know he lives and loves us.

Just as athletes and singers, speakers and performers on stage seek to bring themselves to the maximum degree of concentration and relaxation by deep, rhythmical breathing, so we can learn from them how to sit quietly and breathe properly.

Follow your breath down deeply within you, trying to relax as the flow of energy courses through your being, giving you new life and energy. When a basic rhythm of inhalation and exhalation has been established, seek to synchronize your breathing with the reverent repetition of the Jesus Prayer. As you breathe in, mentally say: "Lord, Jesus Christ." As you breathe out, say: "Son of God." Breathe in again as you say: "Have mercy on me." And, finally, breathe out with the words: "A sinner." Then the process is repeated.

If you are a beginner in prayer, you can accompany such a recitation with simple reflections about the life of Jesus. If you have developed over years of mental prayer a deep awareness of the Lord's indwelling presence, you should not be concerned with ideas, images or any thought process.[15]

Turn deeply within and find Jesus Christ sending his Spirit of love upon you. It is he who will teach you in a nonverbal way how to know the Father and his oneness with Jesus, the firstborn of the Father. You are concerned with experiencing the salvific power of Jesus working upon your unredeemed self, not through a concept about Jesus as Savior, but by exposing your sick self to his healing power. *Jesus* in Hebrew means *Savior*. *Savior* means *Healer*, the one who possesses full life and who can give you a share in this fullness. "And of his fullness we have all received" (Jn 1:16).

Only if we can experience, through the power of the revealing Spirit of Love, our illness and inability to love in return for so much love received from God, can we possibly cry out to be healed. The same Spirit instills into us a confidence and childlike trust that the Father will give us what we ask in Jesus' sacred name: "I tell you most solemnly, anything you ask for from the Father, he will grant in my name" (Jn 16:23-24). Jesus reveals the Father, and the Spirit instills within us the childlike confidence to believe that the Father truly will bestow the healing that we need. "Ask and it will be given you; search and you will find; knock, and the door will be opened. . . . What father among you would hand his son a stone when asked for bread? . . . If you, then, who are evil, know how to give your children what is good, how much more will the heavenly Father give the Holy Spirit to those who ask him!" (Lk 11:9-13).

We will begin gradually to experience what Peter preached in *Acts,* that there is no other name whereby we are to be saved. In a car accident one can cry out in need to be saved: "Jesus Christ, help me!" We should also be able to cry out continually in deep prayer and then to experience the effect of such a heartfelt prayer. Jesus alone can bring health. This name that brings life should be on our lips day and night.

Pronouncing the name of Jesus allows us to make his prayer our own and to enter into a greater sharing in his priesthood. This way of prayer is not a selfish "Jesus-and-I" piety. To the degree that we experience the tremendous love of God in Jesus Christ, we can let this love pour out to every man and woman, brother and sister. We cannot run to all parts of the world to bind up the wounds of the sick of body or assist the mentally disturbed, but in deep prayer before the throne of the Father we can exercise the healing power of Jesus Christ. We render Jesus Christ present again in the world in his priestly action of offering the whole world, healed and restored, back to his Father in praise and thanksgiving.

BRINGING CHRIST TO BIRTH

Jesus Christ waits for us to pronounce his name and render him again present and localized in the world. Jesus is the Incarnate Word, the plenitude of God's speech. Mary, the mother of God, first pronounced his name, and he became man, our brother. We, too, have this awesome power, given in embryonic form in baptism, a power that increases each time we utter his sacred name consciously and with reverence and love. We render Jesus Christ present in a new and wonderful way. The world will be little aware of his presence if we are of little faith. As we pronounce this name, we will experience more and more that which Paul prayed all Christians might know:

> Out of his infinite glory, may he give you the power through his Spirit for your hidden self to grow strong, so that Christ may live in your hearts through faith, and then, planted in love and built on love, you will with all saints have strength to grasp the breadth and the length, the height and the depths; until, knowing the love of Christ, which is beyond all knowledge, you are filled with the utter fullness of God (Eph 3:16-19).

Jesus is seeking admission into the hearts of all men. If we cry out in true sincerity, "Lord Jesus, have mercy!" then the words of *Revelation* will come true: "Look, I am standing at the door, knocking. If one of you hears me calling and opens the door, I will come in to share his meal, side by side with him" (Rv 3:20).

THE TRANSFIGURING LORD

Jesus is the transfiguring Lord. He first transfigures us, bathes us in the Taboric light. It was this light that the Greek Hesychastic Fathers experienced as the enveloping, uncreated energies of the Son and the Spirit assimilating them into divinized beings, one with the Father in Jesus through his Spirit. Jesus wishes to transfigure the whole world through us, by our humble actions in the world. He fills all things: "the fullness of him who fills the whole creation" (Eph 1:23). By pronouncing the holy name of Jesus we release this transfiguring power. We call him into being to touch a world groaning in travail. We ask him to transform the universe, to make each human being, each part of God's creation into members of the Body of the Risen Lord. In such prayer, redemption is experienced as the process by which Jesus Lord transfigures the world through other loving human beings who allow him to have his redeeming way in them. They sing with him the *Hymn of the Universe;* they celebrate, using the raw stuff of their daily, monotonous lives, Christ's Mass over the world.

This world is not to be annihilated; it is destined to be transfigured into Christ. The Body of Christ is being formed out of the whole of creation, including not only human beings made according to his image and likeness but also the material, subhuman creation. In pronouncing Jesus' name, we are becoming members of the Body of Christ that is reaching out to the whole universe in order to bring it into his divine life. "The whole creation is eagerly waiting for God to reveal his sons" (Rom 8:19). In this transfiguring process the whole cosmos will bend before the power of Jesus. "But God raised him high and gave him the name which is above all other names so that all beings in the heavens, on earth and in the underworld, should bend the knee at the name of Jesus and that every tongue should acclaim Jesus Christ as Lord to the glory of God the Father" (Phil 2:9-11).

In his resurrection appearances to his disciples, Jesus showed himself in various forms. "After this, he showed himself under another form to two of them as they were on their way into the country" (Mk 16:12). He continues to reveal himself in various forms as the power that is transfiguring this world through us. What higher form of contemplation than consciously to let the transfiguring power of Jesus pour over us and through us to the whole world! What greater sharing in the priesthood of Christ than to pronounce the sacred name that transfigures every person that we meet! We serve them in the name of Jesus. We cry out to the Lord, so that all will reach the fullness of the sons of God. "Come, Lord Jesus, Maranatha!" (Rv 22:20).

The Body of Christ is evolving until all will recognize him as head of the New Creation. Thus we move from petition to praise and thanksgiving; the reverent invocation of the name of

Jesus leads us into the continual celebration of the cosmic
Eucharist of Jesus Christ. ''With desire I have desired to eat this
passover with you'' (Lk 22:15). Jesus celebrates with us his
barakah, his thanksgiving to the awesome, transcendent Father.
And we are given this same power through Jesus Christ to pronounce our *barakah* in praise of the Father. We make Jesus'
prayer ours as we pronounce all day the name of Jesus, the name
that most pleases the heavenly Father.

The name of Jesus leads us to the Holy Spirit. Jesus Christ is
always sending the Paraclete in order that we might understand
in the heart, not only with the mind, all that Jesus has said, all
that he is. St. Paul tells us that without the Holy Spirit we cannot even say the name of Jesus. The Spirit sent into the heart
teaches us to call out, ''Abba, Father,'' to love the Lord with
our whole heart. ''Not by bread alone does man live,'' is a
message taught us in the desert of our hearts by the Spirit who
drives us there. It is one and the same Spirit who hovered over
the chaotic world in the beginning; who hovered over the
Israelites in the desert as the cloud by day and the pillar of fire
by night; who hovered over the Virgin Mary at Nazareth when
she conceived by the Holy Spirit and the Word became flesh;
who hovered over the humble suffering Servant of Yahweh
when he was baptized in the Jordan; who again hovered in the
cloud through which the Father spoke his approving words at
the Transfiguration on top of Mount Tabor, ''This is my Beloved Son in whom I am well pleased''; who hovered over the
mother of God and the disciples at the first Pentecost in the
form of fiery tongues; and who hovers over us with his mighty
power when we pronounce the sacred name of Jesus. As we pronounce that name, the Spirit of Jesus teaches us all we need to
know about him. He pours into our hearts his gifts of prayer,
faith, healing, prophecy, speaking in tongues, adoration and
glory of the Father, reading hearts, and discerning God's ways.
He fills us with his fruits of love, peace, joy, gentleness and
kindness (Gal 5:22).

JESUS LEADS US TO THE FATHER

The chief work of Jesus, both on earth and now in his glorious resurrection, is to reveal the Father to us. "Philip, he who sees me, sees the Father" (Jn 14:9). Jesus is only the Way that leads us to the Father. The Father is greater than Jesus. The Son has his whole reality in being related to the Father. The Word of God has no meaning except in relationship to the One who speaks that Word, namely, the heavenly Father. The Father is eternally well pleased in his Son (Lk 3:22) because he is the perfect Image of the Father. The Father sees himself totally in the Other and loves him in the outpouring of himself to the Other through his Spirit of Love. The Father begets us as his children when we unite ourselves with Jesus. We become children of God and, with Jesus, coheirs of heaven forever (Rom 8:16-17, Gal 4:6).

In leading us to the Father, Jesus brings us into a total presence of God where we can experience him as Love. The sun's rays can flash off a prism and give colored light. The same rays can hit a lens and become concentrated. Not only do they illuminate but they burn with the heat of fire. This is similar to the experience of the continuous repetition, in loving adoration, of the name of Jesus. The presence of Jesus generates a burning love within the heart. A unity that simplifies the whole mystery of God's infinite love in the first creation, the incarnation, redemption and our sanctification takes over and operates in our hearts. Christ, in Paul's words, "live in your hearts through faith, and then, planted in love and built on love, you will with all the saints have strength to grasp the breadth and the length, the height and the depth; until, knowing the love of Christ, which is beyond all knowledge, you are filled with the utter fullness of God" (Eph 3:17-19).

We begin to experience how Jesus gathers all things together. The whole Christ comes to us through the revelation of the Spirit as our Alpha and Omega, our beginning and our end. The mere name is not important. It is the presence that flows from the recitation of the name. Hence the Jesus Prayer is more than an ejaculation, a spiritual opiate to use, as Franny in J.D. Salinger's novel, *Franny and Zooey,* sought to do, in order to "cop out" of society or to run away into a dreamworld of escape and uninvolvement.

As we synchronize his name with our breathing, we will know by experience that he is our breath, our very life. Our "magnificent obsession" becomes the consciousness of his increasing and our proportionate decreasing before his allness. Only the Holy Spirit can lead us into that intimate, mysterious knowledge which Paul wanted to possess: "All I want is to know Christ and the power of his resurrection and to share his sufferings by reproducing the pattern of his death" (Phil 3:10).

THE JESUS PRAYER—A WAY OF LIFE

The Jesus Prayer is ultimately a way of finding life in Christ, the life which St. Paul so dynamically describes in his epistles. This is life in a Person who dwells intimately and deeply within us. He gives us the power to become children of God, to love the Father with his love. We experience grace no longer as a thing, but rather as a relation in love to Persons, to the uncreated energies, Jesus Christ and his Spirit, loving the Father in us. The name of Jesus brings God's presence into our life. His is an active presence of love that continues to love his world through us and to change his creation into a new and transfigured world.

Today we are experiencing the trauma of reexamining the traditional forms of our faith. We must return to the experience of a heartfelt encounter with Jesus, the living Lord. His presence can no longer be for us a mere thing. We can no longer be content to be a subject, adoring a far-off object. We have been freed by Christ's Spirit and are no longer under the law of sin. "Everyone moved by the Spirit is a son of God. The Spirit you received is not the spirit of slaves bringing fear into your lives again; it is the spirit of sons, and it makes us cry out, 'Abba,

Father!' The Spirit himself and our spirit bear united witness that we are children of God" (Rom 8:14-16).

The Christified man or woman of the Jesus Prayer moves out into the modern, busy world, filled with love of God and with God's love for his world. Such a person offers himself or herself as a reconciler of the whole world according to St. Paul's vision of the cosmic Christ. Such a Christian seeks to bring Jesus Christ, the Son of God, as Lord, not only in his or her life, but through love and the healing power of Jesus to bring him as Lord to each person encountered. The Jesus Prayer aims to lead Christians to incessant prayer. It still has great meaning for us all. Jesus Christ, the same yesterday, today and always. "Lord, Jesus Christ, Son of God, have mercy on me, a sinner."

7.

INSTANT NIRVANA AND THE DARK DESERT

Studying the language used by the hesychastic Fathers demonstrates that any given school of spirituality demands interpretation if "outsiders" to that *lived* spirituality are to find profitable applications for their own spiritual lives. The desert Fathers wrote from their own experiences which were expressed, however, by common symbols.

Adrian van Kaam, C.S.Sp. describes the symbols used in any spirituality as of two kinds: metaphorical and interrelational. Using the symbol of the vine and the branches, he writes:

> This symbol of the vine and the branches has two aspects: the metaphorical-symbolic and the relational-symbolic. It shows the ineffable mystery of Christ's presence in grace; it shows also the mysterious relationship between Christ and the graced person. [1]

There are two other aspects found in all articulated spiritualities. Any Christian spirituality must be rooted in certain objectively revealed truths of *doctrine,* such as God's love in creating us and the world, the gift of his Son in the Incarnation, grace and the basic nature of man and woman as oriented according to the image and likeness of God toward a mystical sharing in God's very own life. The other aspect is the *theoretical-practical* that expresses such an experience based on God's revealed truth as expressed in the church's doctrines so that future generations may also profit from such experiences.

It is precisely this latter aspect that appears to be the weakest element in the hesychastic spirituality. We have sought to interpret and adapt the experiences and doctrinal emphases of the hesychastic writers so as to present a theoretical-practical teaching that would be applicable to modern spiritual life. In this chapter we shall vary slightly from our usual format of presenting a particular aspect of hesychasm with an interpretation and application, in order to give a teaching of very great importance—a teaching that might be lost if we adhered to the earlier format.

Those of you who have read some of the writings of the hesychastic Fathers or even any of the well-known spiritual writers of the West such as St. Teresa of Avila, St. John of the Cross, St. Ignatius of Loyola, St. Francis de Sales or Thomas Merton, may be, in need, I believe, of teaching in two areas: on the proper use of techniques as aids to prayer, and on what to do in the stages of prayer when God purifies you for greater union with him. We will take the teachings of the hesychastic Fathers concerning these two areas and bring them together in a teaching that should prove to be of help to you in your pursuit of deeper contemplation.

TECHNIQUES IN PRAYER

We have already discussed in a general way the importance in Christian spirituality of using techniques to aid us in making contact with God. We are "whole" persons when we enter into prayer—persons of body, soul and spirit. It is only natural that material aids can help us to move from one level to another in a fuller integration of our total human nature in order to pray more completely as individuals meeting our unique, personalized God. We need signs and symbols drawn from our experiences in the world. Such signs are perceived as filled with spiritual meaning and they act on our consciousness, elevating it to a higher plane of awareness. Such signs as light, darkness, fire and breath have always found a special place both in communal and individual Christian prayer.

We should not be in fear of such techniques if they truly help us to pray better. Christians have always used them the hesychastic Fathers were in total agreement as they employed various aids in prayer. They learned that we all have to quiet our inner, psychic world and this can be done easily by rhythmic breathing. The body, soul and spirit merge into a relaxed "whole" person as God's breath is followed inwardly and outwardly, back and forth. You can concentrate on a burning candle and be powerfully aware of Jesus Christ as the light of the world. A picture of a bubbling fountain can bring the words of Jesus to mind: "From his breast shall flow fountains of living water" (Jn 7:38). You can gaze lovingly at a tabernacle that contains the Blessed Sacrament, at a scene of nature, at an icon of Jesus Christ, Mary or the saints and find the calm that ushers you into a prayerful attitude. Music in church services has always been used as a calming and opening technique leading to prayerful worship.

IMPORTANT PRINCIPLES

Bringing together the basic teachings of the Fathers on the use of techniques (which they never really felt needed articulation, at least in the early church), we must set down some very important principles to guide us in the development of our prayer-relationships with God. We need to keep clearly in mind the distinction between God's freely bestowed grace and our free cooperation in using various techniques to dispose ourselves to receive God in his grace. Then we can examine the specifics of hesychastic techniques and the warnings of the desert Fathers in order that we may be guided in the use of such prayer aids.

Firstly, we must remember that God wishes to give himself to us directly through an immediate experience. This communication is made to a human person, a whole being, an "embodied" being, not to a separated soul or a detached intellect. Therefore, it is most important in prayer and worship that we prepare ourselves through asceticism and psychosomatic techniques to bring our whole being to a point of receptivity or "single-mindedness" to receive God's communication on the highest level of consciousness that we can at that phase of our spiritual development attain.

Secondly, we must recognize that all preparatory acts of asceticism, of self-renouncement, of prayer are prerequisite, necessary *conditions* for a state of union with God through grace. But in the ultimate analysis our best efforts leave us absolutely impotent to reach such a union by our own forces. Union with God is a free and gratuitous gift of God whose bestowal cannot ultimately be dictated by a human will nor be assumed to be given after so long a time of preparation.

Thirdly, we must keep in mind that supernatural grace permeates all of our efforts, but by faith, hope and love, which are given to us by the Holy Spirit when we honestly desire them, our human efforts are elevated to a state that makes operations possible that would, naturally speaking, be impossible.

Finally, if our uses of psychosomatic techniques are truly to help us be transformed into channels of God's life-giving grace, they must conform to the whole plan of salvation as revealed by the Gospel and Christian teaching through the church and the lives of the saints. This gives us the norm by which to judge whether a contemplative is experiencing a physiological high brought on by intense asceticism and intellectual concentration or whether he or she is being moved by supernatural grace. "By their fruits shall you know them." If it is God working in us, he will work in harmony always with his revealed will, manifested in the Gospel and in church teaching. And we who, like Jesus Christ, have not disdained to use our bodies and the things of this earth to touch God, will know that our use of techniques has been a helpful means of approaching God. This will be seen in the type of life we live according to God's revealed word in scripture and in the church's doctrine. Thus, whether we can articulate our prayer-experiences in a theoretical-practical expression or not, if we are truly experiencing God, the metaphorical and relational symbols that we use to describe what we have experienced will confirm the doctrine found in Holy Scripture and the teaching of the church.[2]

DANGERS IN PRAYER

Between the 12th and 14th centuries specific bodily techniques were prescribed in the use of the Jesus Prayer. Ways of
sitting, of holding one's head while gazing down at one's
"heart," of breathing and synchronizing the breath with the
fixed words of the Jesus Prayer became a standard part of the
"hesychastic" literature. Up to this time there had been great
freedom in the use of the Jesus Prayer and the breathing was
recommended in a general manner. There can be no doubt, as
we have pointed out in an earlier chapter, that the Byzantine
monks of the East received influences in this matter from
Muslim mysticism.

With the translation of the *Philokalia* into Slavonic, such
techniques spread throughout the entire Slavic world. Abuses
were mitigated when monks in monasteries were able to test, by
their love and service toward others in the community, their
union with God through the use of such techniques. In the
cenobitic monasteries there was also a greater likelihood of finding good spiritual directors who could control any misuse. But
abuses became widespread among hermits and lay persons who
read the *Philokalia* and followed the prescriptions literally
without any guidance from a holy and learned *staretz* or
spiritual father.

St. Theophan, the Russian recluse, speaks of persons going
insane through practicing the Jesus Prayer. "Insanity can come
from the Jesus Prayer only if people, while practicing it, fail to
renounce the sins and wicked habits which their conscience con-
demns. This causes a sharp inner conflict which robs the heart of
all peace. As a result the brain grows confused and a man's ideas
become entangled and disorderly."[3]

In the early part of the 19th century Bishop Ignatius Brianchaninov also urged caution in the use of the material aids in
saying the Jesus Prayer:

> The monk Basil and the elder Paissy Velitchkovsky say that many
> of their contemporaries harmed themselves by misusing material

aids. And in later times cases of derangment caused in this way were frequently met. In fact they are met even now. . . . One is bound to meet them. They are the inevitable consequence of ignorant, self-directed, conceited, premature and proud zeal, and finally of a complete lack of experienced directors.[4]

GUIDELINES

The true teachers of all Christian mysticism, expecially among the hesychastic Fathers, have always insisted on caution. Visions, voices, levitation, celestial odors, sweet tastes in the mouth and gentle touches by angelic messengers were never to be sought for in prayer. The Fathers were quite unanimous in stressing humility and compunction as the true touchstones of a religious experience, and not psychic phenomena. They themselves, as they opened up their psyche through altered states of consciousness in deeper prayer, knew that there could be subjective deviations in judgment, memory and attention. Voices could be distinctly heard. Visions of the saints, of Jesus Christ, of their beloved deceased could occur. They were very wary that such phenomena never be construed as a sign of sanctity or even of progress in prayer.

The words of St. John of the Cross could easily have been written by the hesychastic writers as well:

> It must be known that even though these apprehensions come to the bodily senses from God, one must never rely on them or accept them. A man should rather flee from them completely, and have no desire to determine whether they be good or bad. The more exterior and corporal they are, the less certain is their divine origin. God's communication is more commonly and appropriately given to the spirit, in which there is greater security and profit for the soul, than to the senses where ordinarily there is extreme danger and room for deception. . . . He who esteems these apprehensions is in serious error and extreme danger of being deceived. Or at least he will hinder his spiritual growth, because, as we mentioned, these corporal perceptions bear no proportion to what is spiritual.[5]

Nicholas Cabasilas, the outstanding Byzantine lay theologian of the 14th century, sums up the universal attitude of the hesychastic Fathers toward extraordinary charismatic gifts manifested in the sense order:

> The soul that is penetrated with the examples of Christ and cooperates with the grace of the sacraments sees itself transformed. And this transformation, which is the true virtue, the true sanctity, resides in the will and in no way in the miracles or extraordinary charisms. [6]

There has been a universal caution among the Eastern Fathers from St. Ephrem to Gregory Palamas in regard to any extraordinary psychic phenomena that had repercussions on the sense levels. [7] All the more caution had to be exercised when psychosomatic techniques were employed.

I have met persons who have turned to the Far Eastern forms of meditation that prescribe psychosomatic techniques similar to those found in the writings of the 14th-century hesychasts of the *Philokalia*. They had encountered very grave difficulties. To pass beyond the superficial levels of our own rationally controlled consciousness in order to enter the innermost core of our being, great discipline, great suffering, tribulations and a living faith vision of a present, loving God are required. As a person passes through layers of psychic experiences, dangers rear up. Repressed material that has been drowned in the unconscious can arise threateningly to disturb one in prayer. Sexual feelings can arise, influencing the whole body. Some meditators have reported that they were transported out of the body and suffered tremendous fears in their efforts to return into their bodies. Others have felt that evil spirits entered into their minds as they yielded in complete passivity to their surrounding presence.

Dr. Elmer Green of the Menninger Foundation of Topeka, Kansas, has studied the inner workings of the human psyche in deep meditation. He reports:

According to various warnings, the persistent explorer in these . . . realms . . . brings himself to the attention of indigenous beings who, under normal circumstances, pay little attention to humans. . . . They are of many natures and some are malicious, cruel and cunning, and use the emergence of the explorer out of his previously protective cocoon with its built-in barriers of mental and emotional substance as an opportunity to move, in reverse so to speak, into the personal subjective realm of the investigator. If he is not relatively free from personality dross, it is said, they can obsess him with various compulsions for their own amusement and in extreme cases can even disrupt the normally automatic functioning of the nervous system, by controlling the brain through the chakras. Many mental patients have made the claim of being controlled by subjective entities, but the doctors in general regard these statements as part of the behavioral aberration, pure subconscious projections, and do not investigate further.[8]

We should, therefore, be extremely cautious if God has led us into a deeper prayer form where we yield more of our own doing to the doing of the Holy Spirit. We must be on our guard that we do not render ourselves vacuously empty. There is a true emptying of our own power to come to know God through our own efforts. But there is a higher, inner activity that absorbs us. It is an active receptivity that now commands our attention. It is a loving waiting on the indwelling Trinity to speak the Word of God in the darkness of faith. It is a stretching forth in deeper, more humble self-surrender to God; God is the center of all our strivings, never ourselves. This is why the Jesus Prayer with its emphasis on compunction and the humble cry for continued mercy can be extremely helpful to keep us in a faith vision of not only the healing power of Jesus but of a constant awareness of our own selfish sinfulness that is always so prone to "use" God in prayer for what we can get from him.

Here are some guidelines in the use of the Jesus Prayer or

any other fixation-type prayer of faith in order that we not fall into abuses:

1. There should be no fear in using the Jesus Prayer or any other similar ejaculatory prayer both in our concentrated prayer time and throughout the day.

2. If we are drawn by a movement of grace to use such a form of prayer over long periods of concentrated prayer and are drawn also to employ psychosomatic methods of relaxing, synchronizing the breathing with the mental saying of a given formula, fixating interiorly on some inner "point," such practices should be done only under the direction of a learned and holy spiritual director who personally had made progress through such a prayer form and manifests such progress in the holiness and humility of his life.

3. We should never simply learn either from a book or from a Zen or Hindu master or even an instructor of TM or Silva-Mind Control such a transcendental type of meditation and then transfer the same technique over to a Christian "mantra." If we do, too much emphasis may be placed on the psychosomatic techniques and not enough upon the proper Christian, doctrinal perspective of God's allness; his indwelling, trinitarian life; the need for the sacraments and the teaching church to guide us and strengthen us; and our own need for inner healing by crying out for God's forgiveness and mercy.

4. The writings of the hesychastic Fathers, especially those found in the *Philokalia,* can be most helpful for persons already advanced in the spiritual life, but the techniques given in the later writers of this spiritual tradition must never be divorced from the total teaching that is so much one with Holy Scripture and the church's tradition of liturgy and sacraments. We must seek always the glory of God and self-surrender to his holy will, and never seek a self-satisfying psychic experience in prayer. Poverty of spirit and humility should be the true test of growth in prayer, not how "high" one gets in prayer.

5. The ultimate criterion of whether the Holy Spirit is operating in our lives is the sincerity that we encounter in our

lives and in our surrendering of our lives to his dominance. This sincerity can be measured not by words alone but by deeds. When we see a godly life lived by a person who claims that such and such a technique has helped him or her to become a better person, we can recognize that the Spirit of Jesus has met that person deeply and has transformed that life by grace from God and by human cooperation.

The desert mystics knew from their experiences that God could touch them in a "holistic" manner. They were being grasped by God and they were very much aware of such *I-Thou* encounters. Such moments of consolation were considered as gifts from God to strengthen the desert athletes in their inner struggle to die to self and rise to Christ. They knew that these moments came upon them suddenly and were independent of any psychosomatic technique. It was God condescending to meet them in their needs and he was as "fire touching wood." The wood could do nothing but burn if it were dry.[9]

THE DARK DESERT

The hesychastic Fathers have much to teach us moderns about how to deal with the deepest purifications that come necessarily to those eager for greater union with God. They knew great consolations could come to the courageous who left everything in order to enter "alone with the Alone" in the desert of their heart. But these consolations, they considered, were given to beginners. All such consolations, especially those that had physical repercussions, had to be transcended or else they became obstacles to the love and service of God.

Nowhere do we find the neat distinction, as in the writings of St. John of the Cross, between the purification of the senses and that of the soul or the dark night of the senses and that of the spirit. There runs through the writings of the desert Fathers not only an *apophatic* language to describe how we can know the incomprehensible God but also a mystical *apophaticism* to describe the dark, inner desert that leads to divinization. It is in studying their teaching on interior purification that we see a synthesis of their own practical experience blending with their scriptural doctrine.

The Greek Fathers start from this view of human nature. Our true nature is our real self, the one seen in scripture as made according to God's own image and likeness (Gn 1:26). We were meant to live in God's presence as in light. Our nature was basically good and God's uncreated energies were always present to God. If there was any darkness in us, it came, not from God or from our nature, but from outside, from the prince of darkness. Nilus, one of the great early monks of the desert, writes about the infiltration of evil into human nature from outside:

> God gave the command to do good and to avoid sin, but opposing powers make us tend toward evil, and it becomes difficult to do this good. These sinful powers are not innate to man's nature, but they are brought in from outside.[10]

St. Macarius likewise sees the need for purification as an uprooting of *passions* that have come to our nature as accidents from an outside force. "Therefore, he who says that the cause of the ignominy of the passions is that they are from nature and not accidents has changed the truth of God into a real lie. As I said above, the immaculate and pure God prepared man's image to his own, but by the jealousy of the Devil death centered into the world."[11]

UNION THROUGH SUFFERING

One basic conviction found in all the hesychastic writings, as well as in the Old and New Testaments, is that "the way of God is a daily cross."[12] Diadochus of Photice summarized this common Christian belief of the desert Fathers when he wrote:

> In the same way as wax unless heated and softened for long cannot take the seal impressed upon it, even so man unless tried

with toils and weaknesses cannot take in the seal of God's power. This is why the Lord says to St. Paul: "My grace is sufficient for you; for my power is made perfect in weakness" while the apostle himself boasts saying: "I will all the more gladly boast of my weaknesses that the power of Christ may rest upon me." But it is written in the Book of Proverbs too: "For the Lord disciplines him whom he loves and chastises every son whom he accepts." Now by weaknesses the apostle means those attacks by the enemies of the cross which continually befell him and all the saints of those days in order that they may "be kept from being elated" as he puts it by the abundance of revelations (2 Cor 12:7) but through being humbled rather stood fast in their attitude of perfection and through frequent humiliations devoutly preserved the divine gift.[13]

The inner struggle to allow God to become truly God was conceived almost universally among these Fathers as a "second" martyrdom,[14] a "white martyrdom." It was only in such trials endured with patience and a constant crying out to God to become one's protector and stronghold against the enemies' attacks that one truly entered into genuine prayer. There could be no authentic prayer of the "heart," on any deep, interior level unless such prayer flowed from humility. And humility was learned, not by studying the qualities of such a virtue, but in the battle. Virtues are acquired through suffering. "He who flees suffering is sure to be parted from virtue, if you desire virtue, give yourself up to every kind of suffering. For suffering engenders humility. Until we have attained true knowledge, we advance towards humility by means of trials."[15]

The importance of tribulations in order to acquire true humility lies in the fact that we must see clearly the futility of our own efforts through fear and attentiveness to our own impotence before we will cry out in complete trust to God to become the Savior. St. Isaac the Syrian links up such humility and spiritual poverty with true prayer. "The man who has learnt the need of God's help, prays much."[16] When we have reached a state of being honest, sincere and humble before God, his mercy then surrounds us and we experience by the Spirit a regeneration into children of God.

DESPONDENCY

The parallel of St. John of the Cross' "dark night of the soul" is found in the writings of the Fathers that deal with despondency and dereliction. Yet, as Irenee Hausherr, S.J., points out[17] the pure darkness of St. John was not likely to have been a concept of the desert Fathers. Their thought, springing from Pseudo-Macarius' theology of "total light," always saw God as light leading man into pure light. Like St. John, they saw the darkness as great, but there was always the presence of light to be found in hope.

Insofar as we have tasted the sweetness of God, to that extent the taste of hell comes to the soul that falls back into the night of the struggle against temptations. Under the symbol of attacking demons, the Fathers saw the two greatest purifications to consist in temptations of despondency and of pride. The first series of temptations were known to the Fathers as *acedia*. St. Isaac describes this inner state of despondency and a feeling of having been abandoned by God:

> Trials to the soul, which come from the rod of the spirit and serve progress and growth, trials through which the soul is taught, tested and brought to spiritual endeavor are the following: laziness, heaviness in the body, infirmity of the members, despondency, confusion of thoughts, apprehensiveness caused by bodily exhaustion, temporary desertion of hope, darkening of thoughts, lack of human help, scarcity of the bodily necessities of life and other similar things.[18]

It is in such a state of temptation that we cry out in humility and fear for the face of God. Everything is dark; the desert is dry and empty. Light has been eclipsed; the way seems uncertain. In spiritual ennui we feel suffocated by immobility, confined, blocked at every turn. We cry out to God for his infinite mercy, yet think that there is no one to hear our cry. In such poverty we begin to believe in our Creator. We search for the presence of God as the only source of reality. God is finally becoming God!

But there are still greater interior sufferings and trials by which to learn true humility and enter into contemplating God as light. These are described by St. Isaac as:

> Trials which God allows to attack men who puff themselves up in the face of God's goodness and who offend him by their pride, are the following: withdrawal of the force of wisdom which men possess, constant presence of a lustful thought which gives them no peace, and which is allowed in them to curb their conceit; quick temper; desire to have everything their own way, to argue, to reprimand others; a heart that despises everyone; a mind gone completely astray; blasphemy against the name of God; absurd and laughable suspicions that they are scorned by people, deprived of the honor due to them, that demons mock them and put them to shame, both openly and secretly by every kind of means; and finally, the desire to be in touch with the world and circulate in it, to talk endlessly and chatter senselessly, to be always in search of news and even of false prophecies, to promise much that is beyond their strength. These are spiritual trials.[19]

Such trials as described by the Fathers are truly a taste of hell. But, regardless of the terms used to describe such a darkness, the message of such spiritual Fathers is: "The remedy for it all is only one—humility of heart."[20] The greatest trials and sufferings that we can undergo during this life are found in the purification of pride. The Fathers know from experience, and we know also from our own experience, that the greatest test of love is to die to self-love and to abandon oneself totally in love of God. Before such a state of complete surrender has been reached, what hellish thoughts must be passed through! What terrifying thoughts of blasphemy and doubts about God's existence! How could he really love me? Jesus is really not truly God but just a man and, therefore, God had not yet proved his love for me! God could never forgive my innumerable sins! I am left alone to battle these dark forces! God has forsaken me! He really is not a God of mercy and love but a terrifying God of vengeance and he has discarded me!

A SPIRITUAL FATHER

Such distortions in the area of despondency and pride can be overcome only by humility and a state of compunction that cries out for God's mercy as we see our own sinfulness. The reaching of the individual into the collective realm of the conscious and the unconscious can be the beginning of living in a world of illusions, created by the "demons" or the forces of darkness that attack from within and from without. We must stand vigilant to all interior movements and be trained to deal with the full existential realm of the interior life.

To keep in touch with God's "real" world and to avoid any schizophrenia, the desert athlete recognized the necessity for a spiritual father who would guide him safely between the rocks of Scylla and Charybdis. Obedience to the spiritual father was considered one of the best signs of the operation of humility, offsetting temptations to dereliction or haughty pride. Isaac the Syrian exhorts the hesychasts: "Therefore follow the advice of a man, who has himself experienced all, and knows how to judge patiently what needs discrimination in your case and can point out what is truly useful for you."[21]

The Christian contemplative, in order to move progressively into greater conscious awareness of the indwelling Trinity and unlock the inner mysteries revealed by the awesome, transcendent God, needs to be able to discern the authentic workings of the Holy Spirit from the evil spirits, the "demons," that so easily introduce "tares" where the Divine Sower sowed only good seed, that bring darkness where by nature man is made to reflect the inner light of God's glory. The spiritual father in the Christian tradition, beginning with the hesychastic Fathers of the desert, receives his title because he is a "Spirit-filled" person, capable from his own experiences of traversing the circuitous ways of the interior life. Using his knowledge of human nature and the study of Holy Scripture and the teachings of the church, the spiritual father brings the disciple into the life of the Spirit.[22]

The greatest function of the spiritual father is to warn the disciple against the pitfalls of the inner world and to encourage him against the temptation toward despondency. For this work only one who has gone forth ahead and knows from experience how to discern the workings of the evil spirits, an art that cannot be learned except through personal experience, can be trusted. St. Symeon the New Theologian insists on the necessity of having a truly Spirit-filled director and then on obeying him absolutely. In choosing a guide, one is to look to his virtues, especially expecting to see in him humility, no trace of sensuality, no worldly ambition, no passions, a deep contemplation of the divine light shown in interior wisdom of Holy Scripture, reading the hearts of penitents, and above all, love of neighbor.[23]

FROM DARKNESS TO LIGHT

Even with the help of an expert spiritual guide, we must enter into the inner battle alone and remain there in a state of deep abandonment, cost what it may in personal agony. Only by a complete self-abandonment to the mercy of God can we stifle and repel the desire to be free from such sufferings and abandon ourself completely to whatever God sends, even if it should be greater suffering. Evagrius gave the advice that all Eastern Fathers would repeat to any disciple facing great, inner trials:

> In time of temptations do not leave your cell, inventing some well-sounding excuses; but sit within and endure, courageously meeting all the assailants, especially the demon of despondency, who indeed is the most grievous of all, but who, more than all, makes the soul experienced. If you flee or avoid the struggle,

your mind will remain inexperienced, timid and easily turned to flight.[24]

Such advice was founded on the teaching of St. Paul: "You can trust God not to let you be tried beyond your strength, and with any trial he will give you a way out of it and the strength to bear it" (1 Cor 10:13). Isaiah the prophet also exhorted the people of God to trust in God through all darkness:

Let anyone who fears Yahweh among you
listen to the voice of his servant!
Whoever walks in darkness,
and has no light shining for him,
let him trust in the name of Yahweh,
let him lean on his God (Is 50:10).

Much has to be demythologized in the language of the hesychastic Fathers. But their teaching on the need for *constant* purification needs little interpretation. If we wish to enter into an ever-increasing awareness of loving union with the triune God, then we must expect a lifetime of dying to self-centeredness. We must surrender to God's complete control on all levels of human existence. This means that the love of God is discovered and experienced to the degree that we empty ourselves of all that may impede a total surrender in trusting love to God.

This is a movement toward the true self in an ever-increasing integration in Christ. This purifying process is a continued dying to selfishness and a simultaneous rising from darkness into light and glory through a more intense love relationship to God.

The message of the desert Fathers is consistent with that of all other subsequent Christian mystics of East and West. True contemplation is loving union in a self-sacrificing community of Father, Son and Holy Spirit that, through purification, allows the contemplative Christian to be godly in the same love and humble service toward all others. Darkness and death can only lead to light and life in the Christian vision where prayer is synonymous with purified love.

St. John of the Cross articulates what the desert Fathers lived but in their apophatic mysticism humbly refused to explain. For they knew, with St. John of the Cross, that for those who consented to die to darkness, God was light and they also were light. Only experience could teach that.

O living flame of love
That tenderly wounds my soul
In its deepest center! Since
Now You are not oppressive,
Now Consummate! if it be Your will:
Tear through the veil of this sweet encounter!

O sweet cautery,
O delightful wound!
O gentle hand! O delicate touch
That tastes of eternal life
And pays every debt!
In killing You changed death to life.

O lamps of fire!
In whose splendors
The deep caverns of feeling,
Once obscure and blind,
Now give forth, so rarely, so exquisitely,
Both warmth and light to their Beloved.

How gently and lovingly
You wake in my heart,
Where in secret You dwell alone;
And in Your sweet breathing,
Filled with good and glory,
How tenderly You swell my heart with love.[25]

8.

TRANSFORMING LIGHT

One of the much-loved popular saints in Russia is St. Seraphim of Sarov (1759-1833). His life radiates a simplicity and joy that all Christians should find attractive. This simplicity and joy grew out of his intense, mystical union with the indwelling Trinity. He is an "icon" of the hesychastic spirituality and the perfection of the Christian life.

In a rather famous "Conversation" with his spiritual disciple, the layman Motovilov, Seraphim wants the disciple to see the results of the inner process of divinization that is taking place at all times within the devout Christian. He wishes his disciple to give witness to "acquiring the Holy Spirit" through praying the name of Jesus. As Motovilov looked at St. Seraphim while they sat in the snowy woods of Sarov, the face of the holy *staretz* (spiritual father) began to shine with a light that his spiritual son describes:

> [It was as though you see] the sun's orb, in the most dazzling brightness of its noonday shining, through the face of the man talking to you. You can see his lips moving, the expression in his eyes, you hear his voice, you feel his arms around your shoulders, and yet you see neither his arms, nor his body, nor his face, you lose all sense of yourself, you can see only the blinding light which spreads everywhere, lighting up the layer of snow covering the glade, and igniting the flakes that are falling on both.[1]

What was within both the spiritual teacher and the pupil flashed out in a visible light to bathe both of them in God's glory. St. Paul succinctly describes the end of the Christian life in similar terms:

And we, with our unveiled faces reflecting like mirrors the brightness of the Lord, all grow brighter and brighter as we are turned into the image that we reflect; this is the work of the Lord who is Spirit (2 Cor 3:18).

THE SHEKINAH OF GOD

The *Shekinah* is God's glory or radiant presence as he wishes to share his very own self or his life with us. Throughout the Old Testament, God is present as communicating power coming down to dwell and protect his people. St. John tells us in his Gospel that this progressive dwelling of God in his powerful glory is fully realized in Jesus: ". . . and we saw his glory, the glory that is his as the only Son of the Father, full of grace and truth. Indeed, from his fullness we have, all of us, received—yes, grace in return for grace" (Jn 1:14-16).

Although the fullness of God's glory blazed forth at all times from the depths of Jesus' being, yet it revealed itself only from time to time as brilliant light and healing power. Still the glory was always there. At certain times, as recorded in the Gospels, this glory was beheld as transforming light, brighter than the sun. In the account of Christ's transfiguration on Mount Tabor in Galilee (Mk 9:1-7; Mt 17:1-8; Lk 9:28-36), the Fathers of the East found a model that described scripturally what was to happen theologically and mystically within the hearts of all Christians as they surrendered themselves to the Spirit of the risen Jesus living within them.[2]

TRANSCENDENT DARKNESS

The hesychastic Fathers knew from Holy Scripture and from their own interior life that God essentially would always remain as darkness to their own puny rational powers. In their brokenness they knew that God could never be grasped or possessed as an object. "No one has ever seen God" (1 Jn 4:12; Jn 1:18; 6:46). Yahweh had told Moses on the mountain, "You cannot see my face for man cannot see me and live" (Ex 33:21).

From our human point of view, God in his complete nature will always present himself in darkness, hiddenness and transcendence. St. Gregory of Nyssa beautifully describes what was commonly taught by the early Fathers in regard to God's utter unknowability by our own powers:

> It is like a perpendicular cliff of smooth rock, rearing up from the limitless expanse of sea to its top that overhangs the sheer abyss. Imagine what a man feels when he stands right on the edge, and sees that there is no hold for hand or foot: the mind feels in just the same way when, in its quest for the Nature that is outside time and space, it finds that all footholds have been left behind. There is nothing to "take hold of," neither place nor time nor dimension nor anything else, nothing on which thought can take its stand. At every turn the mind feels the ungraspable escape its grasp, it becomes giddy, there is no way out.[3]

Still Holy Scripture and their own experience in praying in their heart assured the desert mystics that God could be known, that he was light and his light and glory bathed those who had purified their hearts of all self-centeredness. In a word, they experienced by faith that God, as love, was constantly pouring himself out in energizing relations of love through his Son in his Spirit toward his human children.

LIGHT FROM LIGHT

The end of the Incarnation is precisely that God's divine life may be restored within our inner being by Jesus Christ entering within our souls by grace. This grace or divine life is given initially in baptism when the Holy Trinity comes and dwells in us in a new and ineffable way and we begin a new relationship with Jesus Christ.

God does relate to us and the whole created world through the light of his Son in his Spirit. "I am the light of the world; anyone who follows me will not be walking in the dark; he will have the light of life" (Jn 8:12). Jesus Christ, God's presence made flesh, has come into the world as a light, so that no one who believes in him might remain in darkness (Jn 12:46).

The hesychastic Fathers knew from scripture and their own experiential knowledge of God that, although God was in his essence unknowable by human beings, yet God did communicate himself in knowledge and love to us through what they called "the energies of God." Such energetic relationships to us in love are seen in scripture often as radiant light.

> Eloah is coming from Teman,
> and the Holy One from Mount Paran.
> His majesty veils the heavens,
> the earth is filled with his glory.
> His brightness is like the day,
> rays flash from his hands,
> that is where his power lies hidden (Hb 3:3-4).

St. Basil summarized the doctrine of the distinction between God's essence and his relational energies in these words:

> We know our God from his energies, but we do not claim that we can draw near to his essence (*ousia*). For his energies come down to us, but his essence remains unapproachable.[4]

Such uncreated energies of God in loving relationships to us and the created world are what the Eastern Fathers understood to be *grace* in its primal meaning. They are not "things" but they are God in his trinitarian activities toward his created order as he seeks to give himself to mankind.

The end of the whole salvific order as seen by God is that everything created is meant to be reconciled to the Father through the working of his Son through the divinizing power of his Spirit. The redeeming work of the crucified and risen Jesus consists in giving us his Spirit of love through whom we may know the Father and the fullness of the Son (Jn 17:3) and thus we ourselves, by the power of the Holy Spirit, can become truly children of God (Jn 1:12; Rom 8:15; Gal 4:6). "Before the world was made, he chose us, chose us in Christ, to be holy and spotless, and to live through love in his presence, determining that we should become his adopted sons, through Jesus Christ for his own kind purposes to make us praise the glory of his grace" (Eph 1:4-6).

The "Good News" of the New Testament is that the awesome transcendence of God, totally unknowable and incomprehensible by our powers, does come down to us and wishes to dwell within us, sharing in an immanent way his very own triune family life with us. God, then, can be really "known" in the experience of faith, given to the little ones of the kingdom of God. He reveals or "unveils" his holy, loving presence to us at every moment through his uncreated energies of love, operating in each event through created matter. All human beings, therefore, are called by God, in the vision of the hesychastic Fathers, to be contemplatives, to live constantly in faith that strips the covering away from the experience of the moment to reveal God's loving, dynamic, energetic presence at the heart of matter.

We can make contact with God who is directly and immediately present to us at all times through his energies of love. Everything is sacred, suffused with the triune presence of a loving Father, Son and Holy Spirit and transforming us into a sharing of their divine light. Light from light, true God (by grace) from true God, begotten by the Father through his Son in his Spirit and destined to grow from glory to glory: this is our dignity as taught and lived by the hesychastic Fathers. "It is the same God that said, 'Let there be light shining out of darkness,' who has shone in our minds to radiate the light of the knowledge of God's glory, the glory on the face of Christ" (2 Cor 4:6).

A HESYCHASTIC DISPUTE

St. Gregory Palamas (1296-1359) came to the defense of the hesychasts living on Mount Athos and practicing the hesychastic type of spirituality that had been attacked by a learned Greek from Italy, Barlaam the Calabrian. Barlaam, heavily influenced by Western Scholasticism, insisted that God could be known only indirectly. To speak of uncreated energies was, in his mind, to introduce a new deity into the Trinity.

St. Gregory of Palamas, true to the long, patristic tradition in hesychasm, came to the defense of the hesychastic monks by developing his teaching concerning the distinction between God's essence and his energies. He insists on the antinomy of the Christian life of prayer that allows both for God's complete, incomprehensible, transcendent nature and for God's communion with human persons in an immanent union:

> The divine nature must be said to be at the same time both exclusive of, and, in some sense, open to participation. We attain to participation in the divine nature, and yet at the same time it remains totally inaccessible. We need to affirm both at the same time and to preserve the antinomy as a criterion of right devotion.[5] .

Barlaam ridiculed the hesychasts of Mount Athos for sitting in a fixed position while gazing on their navel and synchronizing their breathing with the Jesus Prayer. He claimed that they were incapable of contacting God through the use of the body in prayer. That the human body could be the receptacle for grace was an intolerable heresy for Barlaam.[6] The monks claimed that they were able to see God even in this life through what they called "the Taboric light." This is the uncreated energy of the triune God that transfigured Jesus on Mount Tabor and was seen also by the three disciples.

Gregory Palamas composed his *Triads for the Defense of the Holy Hesychasts*[7] in order to refute the attacks of Barlaam and to defend the orthodoxy of the hesychastic spirituality. For Gregory Palamas, it was the most evident conclusion, stemming from the Incarnation and the hesychastic spirituality that began with Pseudo-Macarius, that, once the Logos of God took upon himself human flesh, matter was sacred and the human body could serve as a point of encountering God in his uncreated energies of love. He writes:

> For he becomes one body with us (Eph 3:6), making us a temple of the whole Godhead—for in the very body of Christ "the whole fullness of the Godhead dwells corporeally" (Col 2:9). How then would he not illuminate those who share worthily in the divine radiance of his body within us, shining upon their soul as he once shone on the bodies of the apostles on Tabor? For as this body, the source of the light of grace, was at that time not yet united to our body, it shone exteriorly on those who came near it worthily, transmitting light to the soul through the eyes of sense. But today, since it is united to us and dwells within us, it illumines the soul interiorly.[8]

It was to be the whole human person—body, soul and spirit—who would be able to encounter the divine energies and experientially come to "know" God in the Semitic sense of becoming a sharer in God's very own nature (as Gregory and the earlier hesychastic Fathers constantly quoted from 2 Pt 1:4). The entire world created by God was a "diaphanous" point of man meeting God in contemplation and in creative, loving work.

DISCOVERING THE LOGOS

We have already presented the teaching of the Greek Fathers in regard to the *theoria physica*. John the Evangelist, Justin, Irenaeus, Clement of Alexandria, Origen, Athanasius and Gregory of Nyssa used the Logos doctrine to explain the incarnational activity of Jesus Christ in the cosmos. It was chiefly St. Maximus the Confessor, however, who developed in great detail this mysterious and deifying presence of Christ the Logos in the world.[9] Each creature possesses a *logos* or principle of harmony that reveals to the purified human being the relationship of a given creature to God's total providence or to the total order of salvation as that principle is related to God's cosmic principle of harmony, his *Logos*.

According to Maximus, after purification we move to a contemplation of the world about us. This world brings us to the inner world beyond the sensible, beyond the phenomena. It is
here that we encounter the mind of God. At this point we pass
from self-activity to become the subject of divine infusion. Such
a discerning is poured into us by the Holy Spirit to "intuit" the
"insideness" of each creature and each event in the Logos.

TRUE THEOLOGY

The highest stage of contemplation and the goal of every
Christian is a mystical contemplation of the Holy Trinity which
Maximus calls *theoria theologica*. In this highest type of contemplation we must progress farther and farther from earthly
thoughts as we become gradually assimilated to God. This is, according to the theological anthropology of the Greek Fathers, to
develop by grace the imageness within us into the likeness of
Jesus Christ. The principle that guides all theory of contemplation and divinization (*theosis*) in the Christian East is that like
can be known only by like. True knowledge of the Trinity can be
given to us only in the proportion that we are assimilated in the
likeness of God. This is salvation in the fullest sense. It is our
restoration to the integrity in which God created us and which
he wished us to possess. Now God no longer reveals himself
through creatures or the *logoi* in creatures, but in his own
trinitarian life of active love dwelling within us.

Sin has separated and divided all of creation into an-
tithetical divisions. Contemplation, especially of the transfiguring love of the Holy Trinity dwelling within us, brings together
all such divisions by the power of the Holy Spirit. The last
separation between infinite God and finite creation is removed
by this highest form of contemplation wherein the trinitarian
energies are seen mirrored forth, not only within the "heart" of
the individual, but in each material creature or event. Vladimir
Lossky summarizes the doctrine of hesychastic contemplation,
"In his way to union with God man in no way leaves creatures

aside, but gathers together in his love the whole cosmos disordered by sin, that it may be transfigured by grace."[10]

INTERPRETATION

How can we interpret the doctrine of the transformation of the material world through contemplation of the inner light of God's presence in a way that makes sense and is also applicable to modern life? We can only penetrate into the vision of the hesychastic Fathers if we understand their dynamic view of God and man in a continuous process of interpenetration through self-sacrificing love. Basically, theology for them is to experience God's love, coming to us constantly through the creative power of his Logos-made-flesh and the divinizing love of the Holy Spirit. Theology is to participate in God's inner, trinitarian life that can only be experienced in loving adoration.

Theology is a life in God's life that, through an experiential knowledge given by the Spirit, allows us to live in the tension of God as transcendent yet immanent. The mystics of the desert knew from the objective revelation in Holy Scripture that God will always be transcendent, "above" and totally undefinable. His awesome totality of being forbids any ultimate objectification on our part. He is a consuming fire (Heb 12:29) that puts to smoke our weak attempts to conquer him by our rational game-playing. They approached him, pure Being, as light inextinguishable.

"God is light, there is no darkness in him at all" (1 Jn 1:5). His presence is always beyond us, as the sun is beyond our grasping and possessing. Yet his light, like rays, shines down upon us at all times. The Fathers knew that precisely because God was so transcendent, perfect, holy and completely self-contained, so also was he immanently present to them.

The bridge that linked God's transcendence and immanence, his "beyondness" and his "nearness" to us, was Jesus Christ, the Word-made-flesh and revealed to us as the way "up" to the transcendent Godhead and as the way "down" into ourselves and the entire, material world to find the triune God at the heart of matter.

THE ETERNAL NOW

Because most of us are not as contemplative as the hesychastic Fathers, we tend to view the unfolding of our lives through historical time and space in three dimensions. Thus time, past, present and future, and space, length, breadth and depth are the square boxes into which we divide all of our human experience, including our relationship with God. That God is Love and Life is soon diluted to "God before creation," "God during creation," and "God after creation." Our response to Divine Love's invitation is soon measured exclusively by extrinsic rules or moral laws of conduct and we lose contact with God's continued and exciting process of always giving himself to us in his uncreated energies of love.

Because they were so rooted in scripture and experienced the Word of God as a living Word revealing the Father's infinite love through his Spirit, the Eastern Fathers had the unique quality of piercing through spatial and temporal concepts by viewing the history of salvation, man's relationship to God, not from our myopic point of view, but from the all-encompassing view of God Almighty. This fourth-dimensional perspective viewed God's transcendent and immanent activities as a unity even though they unfold in time and space. They have unity due to the same love that remained constant. The Fathers realized that it was God's infinite love that initiated the first act of creation, and it is the same dynamic, divine love that evolves this initial creation into the fullness of his plan when the whole universe is to be finally reconciled into the "new creation" foretold by St. Paul (2 Cor 5:17-19).

A modern thinker, Teilhard de Chardin, was aware of this perspective of the Greek Fathers.[11] For both Teilhard and the early Greek Fathers, the same act of infinite love of the Trinity toward us was unfolding in the creation, Incarnation and redemption and will be unfolding in the final consummation of the total universe.

A PROCESS OF TRANSFIGURATION

The prayer of the heart for the hesychastic Fathers was an entire way of living and experiencing God inside themselves and outside in all creation. They knew and experienced through prayer a constant oneness with the loving mind of God. At the heart of reality was a process of transfiguration. All creation, insofar as it is created and immersed in matter, is "transfigurable." It is not complete, nor has it reached its fulfilled "logos," but it is interlocked in a dynamic process of interrelationships with the entire material world around it. We human beings, above all material creatures, are gifted by God with the "image and likeness" of God himself so that we are able to communicate with the mind of God through his Logos and commune with God through his Spirit of love. We are "unfinished" and have the freedom to surrender to the transfiguring process of God's self-giving and thus move the rest of the created world into completion by our loving cooperative work.

God's divine life of the Trinity has been given to us in baptism as an embryo, a tiny seed of life. The process of actuating, with our unique, free cooperation, the divine life within us is a transfiguration that takes place slowly over the long years of our human existence on earth. It is being *now* effected by God's inner activity and our cooperation as we seek to surrender to the divinizing power of the Spirit of the risen Jesus living within us. As the desert Fathers died to their own self-containment, they experienced a new oneness with the trinitarian, indwelling community. They experienced these inner, uncreated energies of love as personalized in the love of a Father, begetting them as sons with God's only begotten Son, Jesus Christ, through the Holy Spirit.

St. Nil Sorsky (+ 1508), who brought Byzantine hesychasm from Mount Athos to Russia, writes in his *Ustav* or Rule:

> When the soul undergoes such spiritual activity and subjects itself to God and through direct union approaches the Divinity, it is enlightened in its movements by an intense light and the mind experiences a feeling of joy of the happiness that awaits us in the life to come. Then an indescribable sweetness warms the heart, the whole body feels its repercussions and man forgets not only any given passion, but even life itself and thinks that the kingdom of heaven consists of nothing other than this ecstatic state. Here he experiences that the love of God is sweeter than life and the knowledge of God sweeter than honey. [12]

For the hesychastic Fathers, the Christian life is considered a growth in that inner trinitarian life through a steady transfiguration. For this reason, not only liturgically but mystically in their prayer life, the feast of the Transfiguration of Jesus on Mount Tabor always played a central part in their life. [13] Christ's resurrection highlights his victory over death and the promise that he holds out to all of us that we may even now share in his new life. The mystery of the Transfiguration is a mystical model that not only professes but actually becomes an experience of Jesus' humanity as the prism that gives us a glimpse of the indwelling Divine Light within him as the true Son of God. It also calls us into a sharing of that transfiguring, Divine Light that shines from within us in its trinitarian life. It also is an inchoative, eschatological experience of the future of ourselves and the entire cosmos as already coming under the transforming power of Jesus Christ, the Pantocrator of the universe, who will bring us and the whole universe into a fulfilled oneness.

This is summarized in the liturgical texts sung in the Byzantine Office for the feast of the Transfiguration, especially the following:

> O Christ God, when you willed to prefigure your resurrection, you chose three disciples, Peter, James and John, and went up

with them to Mount Tabor. At the moment of your transfiguration, O Savior, the mountain was flooded with light and your
disciples fell with their faces to the ground, for they could not
bear the sight of your countenance upon which no one may look,
O Word! Angels attended with trembling and awe, the heavens
were afraid and the earth shook to its very foundations when
they saw the Lord of Glory come upon the earth.[14]

THE LIGHT OF CHRIST

The hesychastic Fathers, so rooted in the New Testament,
continually employed the symbol of light to refer, not only to
Jesus Christ's divinity, but also to his transforming power
through his Holy Spirit to lead us into the divinization process
whereby we can become by grace what he is by nature, light
from light, children of God from God. Light was a fitting image
to convey the mystery of God as one light shared equally by the
three Persons of the Trinity and yet each Person shining forth a
unique ray of that light. This symbol accentuates at the same
time the transcendent quality of God and also the divinizing
power through God's immanent presence within us and the entire material cosmos. Nothing can be hidden from the reality of
God's "raying" love toward his creatures. Yet God is beyond
any thought or controlled imagining on our part.

St. Symeon the New Theologian admirably captures the
transcendence of the Trinity as Light:

> The Light is the Father, the Light is the son, the Light is the Holy
> Spirit: unique light, atemporal, without division or confusion,
> eternal, uncreated, without quantity, no failing, invisible, out-
> side of and above all things in the domain of the real, like that of
> thought that no man has been able to contemplate it before be-
> ing purified, nor receive it before having contemplated it.[15]

Yet these Fathers knew through faith that Jesus, the Light
of the world (Jn 8:12;9:5), was shining within them and trans-
radiating them into light also. His light was shining day and
night within their hearts and in their intelligence. It bathed
them in his radiance and knew no setting. It was living and life-

giving and transforming into light those whom his light enlightened. The desert Fathers believed they were truly *phosphoroi*, bearers of the true Light.

Each day these Byzantine hesychasts sang the ancient vesper hymn, *Phos Hilaron:*

> Hail, gladdening Light, of his pure glory pour'd
> who is the immortal Father, heavenly blest,
> holiest of holies, Jesus Christ, the Lord.
> Now we are come to the sun's hour of rest,
> the lights of evening round us shine,
> we hymn the Father, Son and Holy Spirit divine.
> Worthiest art thou at all times to be sung
> with undefiled tongue,
> Son of our God, giver of life, alone!
> Therefore in all the world thy glories, Lord, they own.

It was a life of pushing themselves through the faith of the Spirit into the darkness of their own interior brokenness. There these athletes of the desert called out for the healing and transforming power of Christ as Light brought to the body, especially to the face. We read in the *Life of St. Antony:*

> For as his soul was free from disturbances, his outward appearance was calm; so from the joy of his soul he possessed a cheerful countenance, and from his bodily movement could be perceived the condition of his soul, as it is written: "When the heart is merry, the countenance is cheerful, but when it is sorrowful, it is cast down" (Prv 15:13). . . . Thus Antony was recognized; he was never disturbed for his soul was at peace; he was never downcast for his mind was joyous.[16]

It was the whole person that was to be divinized by the inner Light of the indwelling Jesus. Jesus was to bring that person into a real sharing of his whole, transfigured humanity-divinity which would affect also the human body of the hesychast. St. Maximus the Confessor put it succinctly, "Man's body is deified at the same time as his soul."[17] St. Gregory Palamas also gave the experience of the hesychastic Fathers when he wrote:

In the same way as the Divinity of the word Incarnate is common to soul and body . . . so, in spiritual men, is the grace of the Spirit transmitted to the body by the soul as intermediary, and this gives it to experience divine things and allows it to feel the same passion as the soul. . . . Then the body is not driven any more by bodily and material passions . . . but turns on itself, rejects all relation with evil things, and itself inspires its own sanctification and an inalienable deification. . . .[18]

TRANSLUCENT ICONS

The Greek Fathers taught that the whole human being has been made "according to the image and likeness" of God (Gn 1:26). The whole person, therefore, including the human body, is an *icon* (*image* in Greek) of God. As the body is a material "place" or *locus* where God's transfiguring light is shining through and divinizing the whole person in the process, so the Fathers extend the idea of *icon* to include all of the created world. Everything material, therefore, can be a "diaphanous" point of encountering the inner, transforming energies of divine love, bringing all things into Jesus Christ.

The *iconic* quality of each material creature to present the insideness of God's presence as transforming love is brought out clearly in *The Way of a Pilgrim:*

The prayer of the heart gave me such consolation that I felt there was no happier person on earth than I, and I doubted if there could be greater and fuller happiness in the kingdom of heaven. Not only did I feel this in my own soul, but the whole outside world also seemed to me full of charm and delight. Everything drew me to love and thank God: people, trees, plants, animals. I saw them all as my kinsfolk, I found in all of them the magic of the name of Jesus.[19]

For the Eastern Fathers matter could never be evil in itself. It comes from God and can serve as a touchstone for contact with God who in his uncreated energies of love sustains and transforms all creation into a sharing of his life in the Body of

Christ. The whole universe is, for those who possess purified eyes, a living sacrament, in the broadest sense of the word. In the meeting of the contemplative and God, the material creation not only symbolizes God's presence but also plays a role in the transfiguring power of God and the contemplative to bring all things into Christ.

This is why Eastern Christians from earliest times up to the present have venerated icons or sacred paintings done in the approved, sober and hieratic manner common to iconography through the centuries. What makes the icon different from other secular or even other religious art is the transfiguring characteristic found in Eastern icons. As the power of the Holy Spirit shone forth from the transfigured Christ on Mount Tabor, so also the human figures radiate a divine presence.[20] St. John Damascene writes: "Matter is endued with a divine power through the prayer made to those who are depicted in image."[21]

The icon is an example of the transfiguration of matter by the Divine Spirit and by human persons, both the instrument, the iconographer, and the person praying before the icon. The transfigured quality of both the icon and the person of faith anticipate and indicate the ultimate transfiguration which is to come in the fullness of time (the *pleroma*) when the cosmos will be transfigured by the power of God who is "all in all" (1 Cor 15:28). The optimistic Eastern Christian view of the world does not ignore the reality of a world that is still groaning in travail (Rom 8:22), but it professes and enters actively into a prayerful experience of God's transfiguring energies of love already effecting what is hidden in embryonic form. The energy is hidden within. Prayerful cooperation on our part with God's creative Word is to bring about the fulfillment of the universe which will be a perfect diaphany of God's indwelling, loving presence within all things.

APPLICATIONS

We, too, in our baptism have been given a share in the very

life of the Trinity. This is the *Good News* that we have heard preached in the church community. The kingdom of God is truly within us. God's immense, self-emptying love has given us his only begotten Son, Jesus Christ, who has died for us, has risen from the dead and now lives in us through his Holy Spirit. By his Spirit we can know by faith that Jesus truly lives in us with his Father. The same glory that transfigured Jesus on Mount Tabor lives within us. Can we ever exhaust "the breadth and the length, the height and the depth" (Eph 3:18) of the love of Jesus which surpasses all knowledge?

His glorified presence dwells within us. We are to grow daily into greater transformation as we yield at every moment to his transfiguring light. We belong to him more and more as we submit at each moment every thought and desire to his dominion (2 Cor 10:5). His divine life courses through our entire being: through all parts of our body, limbs, sexuality, physical senses, emotions, memory, imagination, intellect and will. We are branches and he is the life-giving Vine (Jn 15:1).

As we advance in union with Jesus, we know that something real is happening to us. It is not a physical light that we see within us. It is an inner light having no form, yet "localized" in our *heart,* in the deepest consciousness of our being.

> But if we live our lives in the light,
> as he is in the light,
> we are in union with one another (1 Jn 1:7).

This inner light of Christ makes us forget all sensible, material things or rather it allows us to see also the same light suffusing all creation. It is life-giving, a share already in Christ's resurrection. The eyes of the heart are opened to the Divine Light in all of its manifestation as uncreated energies of love transforming all into a share in God's life. The heart is enlightened and through it the whole being is made lightsome (Mt 6:22). This is summarized by St. Seraphim of Sarov as the peak of the hesychastic life: "When both the intellect and the heart are united in prayer, and when the thoughts of the soul are not scattered, the heart is warmed by a spiritual heat, the Light of Christ enlightens it and fills the interior man with peace and joy."[22]

TRANSFORMING LIGHT

This illumination of the heart flows from an act of the Holy Spirit who is God's divinizing Light. The indwelling Spirit brings us into an illumination that we are really children of God. He effects the likeness of Jesus Christ within us. He is the one who draws out the potentiality locked within us as in a seed to become transfigured into the very Body of the Risen Lord Jesus. This Spirit leads us through the darkness of sin into God's presence as light by instilling into us an abiding sense of sorrow for sins and fear of ever losing the loving mercy of God. Broken in our spirit of egoism and independence, we humbly turn in our poverty toward God. Stripped of the power to heal ourselves, we cry out for healing and the Spirit of love brings this about on the deepest levels of our being, in our "heart."

Our whole being becomes radiant through the effects of this inner illumination. Under the radiation of the divine energies, experienced through the illumination of the Holy Spirit, the energies of the "heart" are vivified in their turn and the inner transfiguration transfigures us into children of God. We have entered into a sharing already, an anticipation, of the future resurrection. Our earthly body has already put on, as it were, the spiritual body. Pseudo-Macarius and his writings had a great influence in developing this teaching of the inner light of the Spirit effecting a partial resurrection that will be completed in the final raising of our mortal bodies to immortality. He writes:

> That heavenly fire of the Godhead which Christians receive interiorly in their hearts now in this life, that same fire which now interiorly directs their hearts, bursts forth upon the dissolution of the body. It again pulls together the members of the body and brings about a resurrection of the dismembered body . . .

for that interior fire, inhabiting our hearts, then emerges and brings about the resurrection of the bodies.[23]

The Spirit witnesses in the depths of our hearts that, in Christ's death, God has condemned sin in the flesh (Rom 8:3). Jesus Christ has passed over from sin and death into a new creation. And we are a part, already glorified, in Jesus Christ risen. His new and glorious life lives within us. In his transfigured state in exalted, risen glory, he draws us through his Spirit into a sharing in that transfiguring process. It is not complete yet; it is ever going on as we yield to the inner light of Christ guiding us through the illumination of the indwelling Spirit. That same Spirit in an ongoing revelation convinces us that God has saved us "by means of the cleansing water of rebirth and by renewing us with the Holy Spirit which he has so generously poured over us through Jesus Christ our Savior" (Ti 3:4-7). This indwelling Spirit of the risen Christ brings us also into the indwelling presence of the heavenly Father who, as Jesus promised, would come with him to abide in us as in a mansion (Jn 14:23).

Freed from sin and darkness by the light of the indwelling Spirit of Jesus Risen, we no longer can wish to live in that former state of darkness. "No one who has been begotten by God sins; because God's seed remains inside him, he cannot sin when he has been begotten by God" (1 Jn 3:9). As the Spirit constantly reveals to us, from within, our true identity as children loved infinitely by a perfect Father through Jesus Christ who has died for us, we can live each moment in his light and with him. We can learn to accept our true identity that is a becoming, a transfiguring as Jesus was transfigured, into the full, matured children of God. But this takes place only in the present *now,* the only meetingplace of the transfiguration as we experience in our *now* moment the eternal *now* of his love for us in Christ Jesus. The Holy Spirit progressively brings about our regeneration as a child of God to the degree that we yield to his illuminations and inspiration, poured forth from within us. We are, according to St. Paul, alive by the Spirit, so we must walk always by the Spirit (Gal 5:16-18).

BRIGHT DARKNESS

The indwelling Trinity shines within us like brilliant rays from the sun. We cannot possess the sun completely, yet the rays do warm us and allow us to bathe in their light. Thus we are not yet completely divinized and surrendered into a oneness with the trinitarian life that lives within us. There is God's light. There is also our own darkness. These two continue all through our earthly existence. At times we "see" the light and follow it. At other times the darkness in us seeks to extinguish the inner light. God's ineffable beauty and glory transfuse us from within. And yet our sinfulness still has need of healing.

One of the most beautiful expressions of this dialectic between the transforming power of God's indwelling light and the areas of our humanity always in need of "reformation" is given us by St. Symeon the New Theologian:

> But, O what intoxication of light,
> O what movements of fire!
> O, what swirlings of the flame in me,
> miserable one that I am,
> coming from you and your glory!
> The glory I know it and I say it is your Holy Spirit,
> who has the same nature with you
> and the same honor, O Word;
> He is of the same race, of the same glory,
> of the same essence, he alone with your Father
> and with you, O Christ, O God of the universe!
> I fall down in adoration before you.
> I thank you that you have made me worthy to know,
> however little it may be,
> the power of your divinity.
> I thank you that you, even when I was sitting in darkness,
> revealed yourself to me, you enlightened me,
> you granted me to see the light of your countenance
> that is unbearable to all.
> I remained seated in the middle of the darkness, I know,
> but, while I was there surrounded by darkness,
> you appeared as light, illuminating me

completely from your total light.
And I became light in the night,
I who was found in the midst of darkness.
Neither the darkness extinguished your light completely,
nor did the light dissipate the visible darkness,
but they were together, yet completely separate,
without confusion, far from each other,
surely not at all mixed,
except in the same spot where they filled everything,
    so it seems to me.
So I am in the light, yet I am found in the middle of the
    darkness.
So I am in the darkness, yet still I am in the middle of the
    light.[24]

A TRANSFIGURED WORLD

As we experience God's transforming light within us, we move in the power of that loving light out into God's created world. God's glory shines out from all corners of creation. What others fail to see, we intuit. We can see with new eyes, transfigured eyes, that show the same uncreated energies of God's love permeating all things.

We place all of our weaknesses with a trusting hope into the infinite allness of God. We open up those creative powers, which we realize can only be the uncreated energies of God's love pouring over, within and through us, to all other creatures that we are privileged to meet and from whom we are to draw out the same loving presence of God.

Love of God becomes truly like the breath of God that combines with our breath as we constantly utter the sacred name of Jesus over the unfinished world around us. We burn to bring forth the love of the triune God throughout the whole universe. Yet we are humbled by our inadequacy. Still we are buoyed up in the faith, hope and love that the Holy Spirit continually pours into our hearts to grasp the present moment and there breathe forth Jesus to that small segment of the world.

Jesus wishes to be transfigured as he was on Mount Tabor, but now in his members. His transfiguring power is given to us. Like Mary, who gave birth to Jesus, we are to bring his transfiguration into actuality by our contemplative action. By pronouncing the holy name and presence of Jesus over the surrounding world, we can release his hidden presence. His glory can radiate through the whole world as we, in the exercise of our royal priesthood (1 Pt 2:9), breathe over the raw material of this universe that is truly becoming the Body of Christ!

We share in the redemption of the universe and become with Jesus Christ "a reconciler" (2 Cor 5:19) of the entire world as we allow Jesus to have his healing, redeeming way in our life. Everything we do is prayer, the prayer of Jesus, as we seek to fashion the Body of Christ out of the material world that we see and touch and reverence for its hidden sacredness.

GOD UPWARD AND INWARD

As Peter, James and John looked up and saw Jesus transfigured in glory, so we look up and "see" by faith, hope and love that Jesus by his Spirit is leading us to the glorious throne of the heavenly Father. We live in a "stretching" action of going home to become more and more "light from light, true God (by grace) from true God."

And yet we also look inward into ourselves and downward into the broken, sordid, unfinished world around us. We tremble at the mystery of God's transforming, self-giving love penetrating and invading us from all sides. We know that life is a continued process of a transfiguration into the light and glory of Jesus Christ.

The prayer of the heart is no longer a prayer of words. It is Jesus Christ as transforming light, bringing us into a oneness with him and his Father through his Spirit of Love.

We live and work in that transfiguring power of Jesus. We know now that what St. Paul wrote is being realized in us, by us and through him in all things: "There is only Christ: he is everything and he is in everything'' (Col 3:11).

True hesychasm leads to the fulfillment of God's creation where there is no more darkness, but only light. It is where rest has replaced restlessness and peace is oneness with God and all creation. Faith and hope bring forth the birth of love that knows no end of continued growth, of becoming ''all in all.'' The spirituality of the hesychastic Fathers leads us into the heart of the triune God, a community of self-surrendering Persons that never knows the word, ''enough.'' It is an experience of the ''moreness'' of God as we open ourselves to the dynamic self-giving of God to us in the ever new beginning of the now moment. T. S. Eliot, in his *Four Quartets,* expresses the process of always beginning and never coming to an end:

> We shall not cease from exploration,
> And the end of all our exploring
> Will be to arrive where we started
> And know the place for the first time.[25]

The words of the prophet Isaiah best lead us to a conclusion of this book on hesychasm and the prayer of the heart. Such prayer is a transfiguration of ourselves and of the whole material world into the light of God. An end will come to darkness and incompleteness and there will be only LIGHT!

> Arise, shine out, for your light has come.
> The glory of Yahweh is rising on you,
> though night still covers the earth
> and darkness the peoples.
>
> Above you Yahweh now rises
> and above you his glory appears.
> The nations come to your light
> and kings to your dawning brightness.
>
> . . .At this sight you will grow radiant,
> your heart throbbing and full
> since the riches of the sea will flow to you,
> the wealth of the nations come to you;

. . .No more will the sun give you daylight,
nor moonlight shine on you,
but Yahweh will be your everlasting light,
your God will be your splendor.

Your sun will set no more
nor your moon wane,
but Yahweh will be your everlasting light
and your days of mourning will be ended.

Your people will all be upright,
possessing the land for ever;
a shoot that Yahweh has planted,
my handiwork, designed for beauty (Is 60:1-21).

FOOTNOTES

INTRODUCTION

1. Cited by Rollo May, *Man's Search for Himself* (New York: Dell Publishing Co., 1953), pp. 276-277.

2. Robinson Jeffers, "Tower Beyond Tragedy," *Roan Stallion* (New York: Random House, Inc., 1925).

3. James O. Hannay, ed., *The Wisdom of the Desert* (New York: Whittaker, 1904), p. 35.

4. Thomas Merton, *The Wisdom of the Desert* (New York: New Directions, 1960), p. 4.

5. St. Isaac of Syria, *Directions on Spiritual Training* in *Early Fathers from the Philokalia* trans. E. Kadloubovsky and G.E.H. Palmer (London: Faber & Faber Ltd., 1954), p. 240.

CHAPTER ONE

1. Rollo May, *Man's Search for Himself* (New York: Dell Publishing Co., Inc., 1953), p. 14.

2. V.E. Frankl, *La Psychotherapie et son image de l'image de l'homme* (Paris: 1970), p. 150.

3. T.S. Eliot, "The Hollow Men," *Collected Poems* (New York: Harcourt, Brace & Co., 1934), p. 101.

4. John Macquarrie, *Paths in Spirituality* (New York: Harper & Row, 1972), p. 4.

5. C.G. Jung, *Psychology and Religion: West and East,* trans. R.F.C. Hull (London: 1958), p. 537.

6. Pierre Adnes, "Hesychasm," *Dictionnaire de Spiritualite* (Hereinafter abbreviated *DS*) (Paris: 1969), T. 7, Col. 384.

7. *Apophthegmata Patrum; Arsenius 1, 2, PG* 65, 88 BC.

8. St. Basil, *PG* 31, 136 BC.

9. St. John Climacus, *Gradus* 27, *PG* 88, 1108 CD.

10. Ibid. 1100 A.

11. For material dealing with the heart as the center of human personality, cf.
A. Guillaumont, "Le 'coeur' chez les spirituels grecs a l'epoque des anciens,"
DS (Paris: 1927), T. 2, 2, Col. 2281-2288;
A. Guillaumont, "Le sens du coeur dans l'antiquite," *Le Coeur; Etudes
carmelitaines* (Paris: Desclee de Brouver, 1950), pp. 41-88;
T. Spidlik, "The Heart in Russian Spirituality," Orientalia Christiana Analec-
ta, No. 195, *The Heritage of the Early Church . . . in Honour of G.V. Florov-
sky* (Rome: Pontifical Oriental Institute, 1973), pp. 361-374;
A. Lefevre, "Cor et cordis affectus. Usage biblique," *DS* (Paris, 1953), T. 2,
2, Col. 2278-2281;
J.B. Bauer, "De 'cordis' notione biblica et judaica," *Verbum Domini,* 40
(1962), pp. 27-32.

12. St. Theophan the Recluse, cited in *The Art of Prayer,* compiled by Igumen
Chariton and trans. by E. Kadloubovsky and G.E.H. Palmer (London: Faber
& Faber, 1966), pp. 190-191.

13. Dr. John Macquarrie uses *focus* in this sense: *Principles of Christian
Theology* (London, 1966), pp. 230 ff, 249-398.

14. For a review of the latest scholarship on this anonymous writer who had so
much influence on Christian piety and for a new translation of his *Spiritual
Homilies* see George A. Maloney, S.J., *Intoxicated with God. The 50 Spiritual
Homilies of Macarius* (Denville, N.J.: Dimension Books, 1978). All future
references to *Spiritual Homilies* will be from this translation.

15. Ibid. p. 100.

16. The most recent translation and commentary on these two works of
Evagrius have been done by John Eudes Bamberger, OCSO, *The Praktikos and
Chapters on Prayer* (Spencer, Mass.: Cistercian Publications, 1970). Irenee
Hausherr, S.J. gives us a French translation and commentary of *Chapters on
Prayer: Les lecons d'un contemplatif: Le Traite de l'Oraison d'Evagre le Pon-
tique* (Paris: 1960) while A. and C. Guillaumont give us *The Praktikos* in
French translation and commentary: *Traite Pratique ou le* Moine in *Sources
Chretiennes,* (Paris: Cerf, 1971), Vol. 170-171.

17. Bamberger, op. cit., No. 60, p. 65.

18. Ibid. No. 61, p. 65.

19. Ibid. No. 64, p. 33. In Greek the phrase is *"to oikeion phengos."*

20. Ibid. No. 69, p. 66. In Greek the phrase is *"he pikeia eremia."*

21. *The Chapters on Spiritual Perfection of Diadochus* are found in Greek and French in *Sources Chretiennes,* ed. E. des Places, Vol. 5 (Paris: Cerf, 1943).

22. Cf. I. Hausherr, "La methode d'oraison hesychaste," *Orientalia Christiana,* Vol. IX, No. 36 (Rome: Pontifical Oriental Institute, 1927), pp. 109-210.

23. There is a good English translation by Archimandrite Lazarus Moore (London: Faber & Faber, 1958).

24. John Climacus, *Scala Paradisis; Gradus XV, PG* 88, 889 D. Many authors translate this text to imply that Climacus was teaching the full, traditional Byzantine Jesus Prayer: "Lord, Jesus Christ, Son of God, have mercy on me, a sinner." Cf. L. Moore, op. cit. p. 154 and note 1 on p. 130.

25. I. Hausherr, S.J., *The Name of Jesus,* trans. Charles Cummings, OCSO (Kalamazoo, Mich.: Cistercian Publications, Inc., 1978), pp. 282-286.

26. John Climacus, *Scala Paradisis, PG* 88, 1112 C.

27. Ibid. *Gradus XXI, PG* 88, 1032 C.

28. Philotheus of Sinai, *Dobrotoliubie* (The *Philokalia* in Russian), No. 22-23 (Moscow: 1888), T. 3, p. 454.

29. The text of Pseudo-Chrysostom can be found in Migne, *PG* 60, 752-755.

30. I. Hausherr has made a translation and commentary of the three methods: "La Methode d'oraison hesychaste," *Orientalia Christiana,* Vol. IX, No. 36 (Rome: Pontifical Oriental Institute, 1927), pp. 109-210.

31. J. Gouillard, *Petite Philocalie de la Priere du Coeur* in *Documents Spirituels,* 5 (Paris: 1953) quotes an anonymous text giving a warning against certain physiological, fake consequences coming from this method which "relies on Islamic fakes and their methods of *dhikr."* Cf. pp. 305-306.
Cf. also M.L. Gardet, "La mention du nom divin en mystique musulmane," *Revue Thomiste* (1952), pp. 642-646;
George Wunderle, "La Technique de l'Hesychasme," *Etudes Carmelitannes: Nuit Mystique* (Paris: 1938), p. 62.

32. St. Gregory of Sinai, *Texts on Commandments and Dogmas,* and *Instructions to Hesychasts,* in *Writings from the Philokalia on Prayer of the Heart* (London: Faber & Faber, 1951), pp. 37-94.

33. Cf. J. Bois, "Gregoire le Sinaite et l'hesychasm athos au XIVe siecle," *Echos d'Orient,* Vol. V (Oct., 1902), p. 69.

34. Patriarch Callistus and Ignatius of Xanthopoulos, *Directions to Hesychasts*

in *Writings from the Philokalia on Prayer of the Heart* (London: Faber & Faber, 1951), pp. 164-273.

35. Cf. G.A. Maloney, S.J., *A Theology of Uncreated Energies* (Milwaukee: University of Marquette Press, 1978) and John Meyendorff, *A Study of Gregory Palamas* (London: The Faith Press, 1964) trans. G. Lawrence.

36. Cf. J. Gouillard, "La Centurie," *Echos d'Orient*, Vol. 37 (1938), p. 459.

37. *PG* 150, 1101 ff. John Meyendorff has edited the Greek text with a French translation, *Triades pour la defense des saints hesychastes* (Louvain: 1954).

38. Cf. G. A. Maloney, S.J., *Russian Hesychasm* (The Hague: Mouton Publishers, 1973).

39. Ignatius Brianchaninov, *On the Prayer of Jesus, from the Ascetic Essays*, trans. Lazarus Moore (London: 1952).

40. R. M. French published an English translation with the same title and includes the second part, *The Pilgrim Continues His Way* (London: 1943).

41. *The Way of a Pilgrim*, trans. R. M. French (New York: Seabury Press, 1965), pp. 88-89.

CHAPTER TWO

1. A. Whitehead, *Process and Reality* (New York: Macmillan, 1929) pp. 519-520.

2. St. Basil, *Epistolae*, XC, LXX and XCII, *PG* 32, 473, 433-36, 480.

3. St. Macarius, Homily 2, trans. G. A. Maloney, S.J. in *Intoxicated with God* (Denville, N.J.: Dimension Books, 1978), p. 34.

4. *Imitation of Christ*, Book One, Ch. 20.

5. St. John Climacus, *The Ladder of Divine Ascent*, trans. Lazarus Moore (London: Faber & Faber, 1959), Step 15, p. 153.

6. Palladius, *Historia Lausiaca*, *PL* 73, 1093.

7. *Writings from the Philokalia on Prayer of the Heart* (London: Faber & Faber, 1951), p. 164.

8. John Macquarrie, *An Existentialist Theology: A Comparison of Heidegger and Bultmann* (New York: Harper Torchbooks, 1955 & 1965), p. 50.

9. *Writings from the Philokalia on Prayer of the Heart*, p. 45.

10. Archimandrite Kallistos Ware, "Silence in Prayer. The Meaning of *Hesychia*," *One Yet Two: Monastic Tradition East and West*, Cistercian

Studies Series, No. 29 (Kalamazoo: Cistercian Publications, 1976), pp. 23-26.

11. St. Basil, *Epistola* 2, *PG* 32, 228 A.

12. St. Gregory of Sinai, *Instructions to Hesychasts* in *Writings from the Philokalia on Prayer of the Heart,* pp. 76-77.

13. T. Merton, *Contemplation in a World of Action* (New York: Doubleday, 1971), p. 36.

14. King James Version.

15. T. Merton, *Contemplation in a World of Action,* p. 126.

16. B. Lonergan, S.J., *Method in Theology* (New York: Herder & Herder, 1972), p. 9.

17. Ibid. p. 9.

18. Ibid. p. 241.

19. T. Merton, *The Climate of Monastic Prayer* (Spencer, Mass.: Cistercian Publications, 1969), p. 128.

20. Evagrius, *The Praktikos and Chapters on Prayer,* trans. and commentator John Eudes Bamberger, OCSO (Spencer, Mass.: Cistercian Publications, 1970), p. 66.

21. St. Ignatius to the Ephesians, 15, Fathers of the Church Series (Washington, D.C.: 1946), p. 93.

22. N. Cabasilas, *De Vita in Christo* 6; *PG* 150; 657-659, quoted by J. M. Hussey, "Symeon the New Theologian and Nicolas Cabasilas: Similarities and Contrasts in Orthodox Spirituality," *Eastern Churches Review,* 4 (1972), p. 139.

23. Evagrius, op. cit. No. 123-125, p. 76.

CHAPTER THREE

1. Boris Pasternak, *Doctor Zhivago* (New York: Pantheon Books, 1958), p. 42.

2. King James Version.

3. On this subject cf. I. Hausherr, *The Name of Jesus,* trans. Charles Cummings, OCSO (Kalamazoo, Mich.: Cistercian Publications, Inc., 1978), p. 126; "Comment Priaient les Peres, *Revue d'Ascetique et de Mystique* (Jan-Mar, 1956), pp. 33-36; "L'erreur fondamentale et la logique du Messalinisme," *Orientalia Christian Periodica,* 1 (Rome: 1935), pp. 328-360.

4. Origen, *On Prayer,* The Classics of Western Spirituality Series, trans. Rowan

A. Greer (New York: Paulist Press, 1979), Ch. 12, 2, pp. 104-105.

5. St. Augustine, *Epist. Class.* 111, 121, *PL* 33, 493-507.

6. St. Basil, *Regulae fusius tractatae, PG* 31, 920C-921B. On this topic of praying always and the doctrine of the Greek Fathers, cf. I. Hausherr, *Hesychasme et Priere* (Rome: Pontifical Oriental Institute, 1966).

7. Cassian, *Conferences* 10, Ch. 7, *A Select Library of Nicene and Post-Nicene Fathers of the Christian Church* (Grand Rapids, Mich.: Wm. B. Eerdmanns, 1964).
Works that deal with the writings and thought of Cassian are:
Owen Chadwick, *John Cassian* (London: University Press, 1968);
John Cassian, Conferences in *Sources Chretiennes,* No. 54 (Paris: Cerf, 1968);
Institutions Cenobitiques in *Sources Chretiennes,* No. 109 (Paris: Cerf, 1965);
Dom A. Menager, "La Doctrine Spirituelle" (Paris: 1923), Vol. VIII, pp. 183-212;
Michel Olphe-Galliard, "Cassien (Jean)," *DS* (Paris: Beauchesne, 1953), Col. 214-276;
Michel Olphe-Galliard, "La Purete de Coeur d'apres Cassien," *Revue d'Ascetique et de Mystique* (Toulouse: 1936), pp. 28-60;
Ibid. "La Science Spirituelle d'apres Cassien," *Revue d'Ascetique et de Mystique* (Toulouse: 1937), pp. 141-160;
Dom E. Pichery, "Les Conferences de Cassien," *La Vie Spirituelle* (Paris: 1921), Vol. 4, pp. 55-66.

8. St. Theophan the Recluse, cited in *The Art of Prayer,* compiled by Igumen Chariton and trans. by E. Kadloubovsky and G.E.H. Palmer (London: 1966), p. 17.

9. St. Isaac of Syria, *Directions on Spiritual Training* in *Early Fathers from the Philokalia* (London: Faber & Faber, 1954), p. 235.

10. John Cassian, *Conferences,* 10, Ch. 11.

11. For a simple use of such "aspiration" prayer used in the West, cf. V. Poslusney, O. Carm., *Union with the Lord in Prayer* (Locust Valley, N.Y.: Living Flame Press, 1972).

12. J. Lotz, *Interior Prayer: The Exercise of Personality* (New York: Herder & Herder, 1965), p. 133.

13. Pseudo-Dionysius, *Mystical Theology,* cited in *The Soul Afire,* ed. H.A. Reinhold (Garden City, N.Y.: Doubleday, Image Books, 1973), p. 49. This author is called Pseudo-Dionysius because he infers in his writings, in order to give them greater authority, that he is the Athenian Dionysius who was converted by St. Paul's preaching in Athens.

14. E. Neumann, *Origins and History of Consciousness* (Princeton, N.J.: Princeton University Press, 1971), pp. 121 ff.

CHAPTER FOUR

1. Paul Tillich, *The Courage to Be* (Boston: 1952), pp. 39-66.

2. Denise Vasse, *Le temps du desir* (Paris: 1973), pp. 19-20.

3. Gabriel Marcel, *Problematic Man,* trans. Brian Thompson (New York: Herder & Herder, 1967), p. 55.

4. Ibid. p. 100.

5. St. Symeon the New Theologian, *Hymns of Divine Love,* trans. George A. Maloney, S.J. (Denville, N.J.: Dimension Books, 1975), Hymn 30, pp. 164-165.

6. A classic work on this patristic theme of *penthos* is the work of Irenee Hausherr, S.J., *Penthos—la doctrine de la componction dans l'Orient chretien* in *Orientalia Christiana Analecta,* No. 132 (Rome: Pontifical Oriental Institute, 1944).

7. Ibid. p. 50.

8. St. Dorotheus, *Doctrine IV,* Nos. 5, 6, *PG* 88, 1665.

9. St. John Climacus, *The Ladder of Divine Ascent,* trans. Lazarus Moore (London: Faber & Faber, 1959), p. 114.

10. Evagrius, *The Praktikos and Chapters on Prayer,* trans. and commentator, John Eudes Bamberger, OCSO (Spencer, Mass.: Cistercian Publications, 1970), Nos. 5, 6, p. 56.

11. Climacus, *The Ladder of Divine Ascent,* Step 7, p. 116.

12. Ibid. p. 115.

13. Cf. M. Lot-Borodine, "Le mystere du 'don des larmes' dans l' Orient chretien," *La vie spirituelle,* 48, *Supplement* (1936), pp. 65-110.

14. St. Gregory of Nyssa, *De Beatitudine,* 3, *PG* 44, 1224C.

15. St. Isaac the Syrian, *Mystic Treatises,* trans. A.J. Wensinck (Amsterdam: Niewe Reeks, 1969), p. 165.

16. Climacus speaks of such tears: "Greater than baptism itself is the fountain of tears after baptism. . . ." *The Ladder of Divine Ascent,* Step 6, p. 114. St. Symeon the New Theologian writes in the same manner: Sources Chretien-

nes Series, Vol. 51, *Theologiques, Gnostique et Pratiques* (Paris: Cerf, 1959), p. 50.

17. St. Isaac the Syrian, op.cit. p. 176.

18. Ibid. p. 330.

19. Ibid. p. 381.

20. *The Way of a Pilgrim,* trans. R. French (New York: Ballantine, 1977), p. 78.

21. C. Marmion, *Christ the Ideal of the Monk* (St. Louis: 1926), Ch. 8; F. Faber, *Growth in Holiness* (Baltimore: 1855), pp. 350-366; I. Hausherr, S.J., *Penthos;* P. Regamey, O.P., "La 'componction du coeur,' " *La vie spirituelle,* 44, *Supplement* (1935), pp. 1-16, 65-83; 45, *Supplement* (1935), pp. 8-21; 86-99.

22. Paul Tillich, "The Eternal Now," *The Modern Vision of Death,* ed. N.A. Scott, Jr. (Richmond, Va.: 1967), p. 103.

23. St. Theophan the Recluse, *Nachertanie Christianskago Nravoucheniya* (Moscow: 1895), p. 145.

24. Pseudo-Macarius, *Spiritual Homilies,* trans. G.A. Maloney S.J. in *Intoxicated with God* (Denville, N.J.: Dimension Books, 1978), Nos. 16, 6, p. 114.

25. On this teaching cf. D. Amand, *L'ascese monastique de saint Basile* (Maredsous, 1949), pp. 152 ff.

26. A saying attributed to Abbot Poemen. *Apophthegmata Patrum, PG* 65, 353A.

27. St. John Chrysostom, *De Paenitentia,* 2, 2, *PG* 49, 285.

28. Thomas Spidlik, S.J., *La doctrine spirituelle de Theophane le Reclus* in Orientalia Christiana Analecta Series, 172, (Rome: Pontifical Oriental Institute, 1965), pp. 147 ff.

29. Climacus: *The Ladder of Divine Ascent,* Step 7, p. 114.

30. Karl Menninger, M.D., *Whatever Became of Sin?* (New York: Hawthorn Books, 1973).

31. Ibid. p. 19.

32. *A New Catechism* (New York: Herder & Herder, 1967), p. 260.

33. Cf. P. Schoonenberg, S.J., *Man and Sin,* trans. Joseph Donceel, S.J. (Notre Dame, Ind.: University of Notre Dame Press, 1965), pp. 129 ff.;

S. Lyonnet, S.J., "Le sens de *eph 'ho* en Rom v. 12 et l'exegese des peres grecs," *Biblica,* 36 (1955), pp. 436-457.
On the concept of sin as a collective and personal evil, whether participated in deliberately or not, but adding to the universal sin in the world, cf.
Bernard Haring, C.Ss.R., *Sin in the Secular Age* (Garden City, N.Y.: Doubleday & Co., 1974);
Sean Fagan, S.M., *Has Sin Changed?* (Garden City, N.Y.: Doubleday & Co., 1979).

34. Bernard Haring, op. cit. p. 28.

35. F. Dostoyevsky, *The Brothers Karamazov,* trans. Constance Garnett (New York: Random House, 1937), p. 317.

CHAPTER FIVE

1. Pseudo-Macarius, *Spiritual Homilies,* No. 21, trans. G.A. Maloney, S.J. in *Intoxicated With God* (Denville, N.J.: Dimension Books, 1978), p. 135.

2. John Cassian, *Conferences,* 18, 13, *PL* 49, 1113.

3. Ibid, 4, *PL* 6-7, 590.

4. Cf. J. Danielou, "Demon dans la litterature ecclesiatique jusqu'a Origene," *DS* (Paris: 1957), T. 3, pp. 152-189.

5. Origen, *Homilia in Josue,* VIII, 4, GCS 7, p. 339.

6. Evagrius, *The Praktikos and Chapters on Prayer,* trans. and commentator John Eudes Bamberger, OCSO (Spencer, Mass.: Cistercian Publications, 1970), No. 48, p. 29.

7. Pseudo-Macarius, op. cit. No. 6, p. 63.

8. This definition is found in J. Muyldermans, *Evagriana,* in the French review *Le Museon,* T. KLIV that gives some recently found fragments of the writings of Evagrius hitherto not edited (Paris: 1931), Fasc. 1, pp. 54, 59.

9. St. John Climacus, *The Ladder of Divine Ascent,* trans. Lazarus Moore (London: Faber & Faber, 1959), Step 15, p. 157-58: "In the rulings made by the Fathers a distinction is drawn between different things, such as attraction, or intercourse, or consent, or captivity, or struggle, or so-called passion in the soul. And these blessed men define attraction as a simple conception, or an image of something encountered for the first time which had lodged in the heart. Intercourse is conversation with what has presented itself, accompanied by passion or dispassion. And consent is the bending of the soul to what has been presented to it, accompanied by delight. But captivity is a forcible and

involuntary rape of the heart or a permanent association with what has been encountered which destroys the good order of our condition. Struggle, according to their definition, is power equal to the attacking force, which is either victorious or else suffers defeat according to the soul's desire. And they define passion in a special sense as that which lurks disquietingly in the soul for a long time and through its intimacy with the soul brings it finally to what amounts to a habit, a self-incurred downright desertion. Of all these states the first is without sin, the second not always, but the third is sinful or sinless according to the state of the contestant. Struggle is the occasion of crowns or punishments. Captivity is judged differently, according to whether it occurs at the time of prayer, or at other times. . . ."

Others who have handled the psychology of temptation development in a similar way are:

Hesychius of Sinai, *De Temp. et Virtute, Cent. 1*, 46, PG 93, 1496C;

J. Damascene, *De Virtute et Vitio*, PG 95, 96;

Mark the Hermit, *De Baptismo, PG* 65, 1013-1021;

St. Nil, *De Monast. Exercit*, *PG* 79, 768B-D;

Peter Damascene, *Philokalia* (Athens: 1957), T. 3, pp. 109-111.

Western asceticism, under the influence of St. Augustine and St. Gregory the Great, has preferred the simple scheme of three stages: suggestion, delectation, consent. Interesting also is a comparison of the *Imitation of Christ* with the scheme of Climacus: 1. simple thought enters the mind; 2. vivid imagination; 3. pleasure or delight; 4. evil motion; 5. consent; 6. enemy enters totally. Book 1, Ch. 13.

10. Macarius gives the example of a merchant sailing with full wind on a peaceful sea. As long as he is not safely in the harbor, he must continually fear lest sudden winds rise up and the waves of the sea threaten the ship's safety. Op. cit. 43, p. 202.

11. Evagrius, *Antirrheticos*, 17, ed. W. Frankenberg (Berlin: 1912), p. 539. Cf. also Nicetas Stethatos, *Cent 1*, 89, PG 120, 893A.

12. Cf. J. Guillet, "Discernement des esprits dans l'Ecriture," *DS*, 1957 T. 3, Col. 1222-1247.

13. The classic work on this is: I. Hausherr, *Direction spirituelle en Orient autrefois* in *Orientalia Christiana Analecta*, 144 (Rome: Pontifical Oriental Institute, 1955).

14. *Life of Antony*, 22, *PG* 26, 876B.

15. Evagrius, op. cit. No. 50, p. 29-30.

16. Ibid. No. 39, p. 36.

17. I. Hausherr has done a learned and definitive article on the origin among

the Fathers of the eight capital sins as found in the Eastern writers. "L'Origine de la theorie orientale des huit peches capitaux," *Orientalia Christiana*, Vol. XXX, No. 86 (Rome: Pontifical Oriental Institute, 1933), pp. 164-175.

18. Evagrius' list can be found in The *Prakitikos and Chapters on Prayer*, No. 6, pp. 16-17.
Cf. Evagrius' doctrine in *Early Fathers from the Philokalia;* Essay to Anatolius, *On Eight Thoughts*, pp. 110-112; *Reflections on the Eight Thoughts*, p. 113; *On Various Evil Thoughts*, pp. 117-124.
St. John Damascene repeats the same list, *PG* 95, 80, as does Pseudo-Athanasius, *Syntagma ad Politicum*, PG 28, 1397D-1400A.
The Latin list of seven capital sins does not include acedia. St. Gregory the Great is the one most responsible for this listing and he begins with pride and then descends to the baser physical sins.
Cf. M.W. Bloomfield, *The Seven Sins* (Grand Rapids, Mich.: 1952).

19. St. John Chrysostom writes: "The Holy Scriptures do not know of any such division. They wish that all lead the life of monks, even if they are married." *Adv. oppugnatores vitae monasticae*, 3, 15, *PG* 47, 373A.

20. Origen, *Fragmenta in Joanne*, IX, *GCS* 4, p. 490, p. 24. Cf. H. Crouzel, *Theologie de l'image de Dieu chez Origene* (Paris: 1956), p. 239ff.

21. St. Gregory of Nyssa, *De Beatitudine*, 4, PG 44, 1241C.

22. St. John Chrysostom, *Homilia de charitate*, *PG* 56, 279-290.

23. St. Symeon the New Theologian, *Hymns of Divine Love*, trans. George A. Maloney, S.J. (Denville, N.J.: Dimension Books, 1975), Hymn 52, p. 263.

24. Cf. I. Hausherr, *Penthos—la doctrine de la componction dans l'Orient chretien* in *Orientalia Christiana Analecta*, No. 132 (Rome: Pontifical Oriental Institute, 1944), pp. 55ff.

25. G. Bardy, "Apatheia," *DS*, Vol. 1, Col. 730.

26. St. Isaac the Syrian, *De Perfectione Religiosa*, ed. P. Bedjan (Paris: 1909), *Logos* 31, p. 197.

27. St. Thomas Aquinas, *Summa Theologica*, I, 77, 2.

28. John the Solitary, *Dialogue on the Soul and the Passions of Men*, trans. I. Hausherr, S.J., *Orientalia Christiana Analecta*, No. 120 (Rome: Pontifical Oriental Institute, 1939), p. 51.

29. Clement of Alexandria, *Stromata*, II, 59, 6, *Sources Chretiennes*, No. 38 (Paris: Cerf, 1954), p. 82.

30. On this point, cf. Jean Danielou, S.J., *Platonisme et theologie mystique*,

Essai sur la doctrine spirituelle de saint Gregoire de Nysse in *Theologie 2* (Paris: 1944), pp. 52 ff.

31. Irenee Hausherr, S.J. has developed this idea in his classic: *Philautie. De la tendresse pour soi a la charite selon saint Maxime le Confesseur* in *Orientalia Christiana Analecta,* No. 137 (Rome: Pontifical Oriental Institute, 1952).

32. Ibid. pp. 141 ff.

33. Cited by William V. Rauscher with Allen Spragett in *The Spiritual Frontier* (New York: Doubleday & Co., 1975), p. 155.

34. Climacus, op. cit. Step 4, p. 81.

35. G. Maloney. S.J., *Reflective Healing* (Denville, N.J.: Dimension Books, 1979).

CHAPTER SIX

1. For a historical survey of how this formula evolved over the centuries, cf. I. Hausherr, S.J., *The Name of Jesus,* trans. Charles Cummings, OCSO (Kalamazoo, Mich.: Cistercian Publications, Inc., 1978), Cistercian Studies Series No. 44;
A monk of the Eastern Church, *The Prayer of Jesus* (New York: Desclee Comp., 1967);
Ibid. *On the Invocation of the Name of Jesus* (Fairacres, Oxford: S.L.G. Press, 1970);
G.A. Maloney, S.J., "The Jesus Prayer and Early Christian Spirituality, *Sobornost,* No. 5 (Summer, 1967), pp. 310-324;
Ibid. *The Jesus Prayer* (Pecos, N.M.: Dove Publications, 1974);
A priest of the Byzantine Church, *Reflections on the Jesus Prayer* (Denville, N.J.: Dimension Books, 1978);
Ignatius Brianchaninov, *On the Prayer of Jesus,* trans. Lazarus Moore (London: J.M. Watkins, 1965);
Mother Maria, *The Jesus Prayer* (North Yorkshire: The Greek Orthodox Monastery of the Assumption, 1975);
Per-Olof Sjorgen, *The Jesus Prayer* (Philadelphia: Fortress Press, 1975).

2. Cf. Igumen Chariton, *The Art of Prayer* (London: Faber & Faber, 1966), pp. 28-29.

3. Cf. *The Prayer of Jesus* by a monk of the Eastern Church, p. 15.

4. Cf. I. Hausherr, "La methode d'oraison hesychaste," *OC,* Vol. IX, No. 36, and "Note sur l'inventeur de la methode d'orison hesychaste," *OC,* Vol. XX (Dec. 1930), pp. 179-182.

5. St. Gregory of Sinai, *Instructions to Hesychasts* in *Writings from the Philokalia on Prayer of the Heart* (London: Faber & Faber, 1951), pp. 74-75.

6. Macarius and Nicodemus, *Philokalia*, First edition (Venice: 1782). This edition is found in *PG* of Migne, Vol. 147.

7. This does not mean that the Slavic world, especially the Russians, was not familiar with the Jesus Prayer. Nil Sorsky (+ 1508) had brought this practice to Russia from Mount Athos and his hesychastic spirituality was followed by many of the more serious monks in Russia. Cf. G.A. Maloney, S.J., *Russian Hesychasm* (The Hague: Mouton, 1973).

8. This first appeared with the title *Sincere Tales of a Pilgrim to his Spiritual Father* (Kazan: 1884).

9. A German translation by Rheinhold von Walter first appeared, *Ein russisches Pilgerleben* (Berlin, 1926). The first French translation appeared in *Irenikon-Collection,* (1928), no. 5-7, followed by another French translation, *Recits d'un pererin russe* (Nauchatel: 1945). Dom Theodore Bailey, OSB, translated it into English, *The Story of a Russian Pilgrim* (London: 1930), based on the French translation in *Irenikon*. Rev. R.M. French published another English translation that is well known in America, *The Way of a Pilgrim* (London: 1930). He also translated into English the second part, *The Pilgrim Continues His Way* (London: 1943). This is available in one edition (New York: Seabury Press, 1970). Two important volumes have allowed many English-speaking persons to read the hesychastic Fathers in the translation from Theophan the Recluse's *Dobrotolubie*. Trans. E. Kadloubovsky and G.E.H. Palmer, *Early Fathers from the Philokalia* (London: 1954) and *Writings from the Philokalia on Prayer of the Heart* (London: 1951).

10. On the power of breathing to aid deeper interiority, cf. Dr. O.Z.A. Hanish, *The Power of Breath* (Los Angeles: Mazdaznan Press, 1970) and J.M. Dechanet, OSB, *Yoga and God* (St. Meinrad, Ind.: Abbey Press, 1975).

11. From ancient times the practitioners of medicine have studied the relationship between the breathing and other functions of the body and psyche. Cf. F. Ruesche, *Blut, Leben und Seele. Ihr Verhaltnis nach Auffassung der griechischen und hellenistischen Antike* (Paderborn, 1930), pp. 209-265.

12. St. Theophan the Recluse, cited in *The Art of Prayer,* compiled by Igumen Chariton and trans. by E. Kadloubovsky and G.E.H. Palmer (London: Faber & Faber, 1966), p. 71.

13. Ibid. p. 24.

14. George A. Maloney, S.J., *Breath of the Mystic* (Denville, N.J.: Dimension Books, 1974).

15. For reflections on the individual words that make up the traditional Jesus Prayer cf. A Priest of the Byzantine Church, *Reflections on the Jesus Prayer* (Denville, N.J.: Dimension Books, 1978).

CHAPTER SEVEN

1. Adrian van Kaam, C.S.Sp., *In Search of Spiritual Identity* (Denville, N.J., Dimension Books, 1975), p. 66.

2. On this subject of discernment of true, Christian mystical experiences, cf. J. Marechal, S.J., *Etudes sur la psychologie des mystiques* (Paris: 1937), Vol. 1, pp. 252-258; also, Jacques Maritain, *Quatre essais sur l'esprit dans sa condition charnelle* (Paris: 1939), especially Ch. 3, "L'experience mystique naturelle et vie," pp. 131-177.

3. St. Theophan the Recluse, cited in *The Art of Prayer*, compiled by Igumen Chariton and trans. by E. Kadloubovsky and G.E.H. Palmer (London: Faber & Faber, 1966), p. 270.

4. Bishop Ignatius Brianchaninov, *On the Prayer of Jesus, from the Ascetic Essays,* trans. Lazarus Moore (London: 1952), p. 95.

5. St. John of the Cross, *The Ascent of Mount Carmel,* Bk. II, 2-3, in *The Collected Works of St. John of the Cross,* trans. Kieran Kavanaugh, OCD and Otilio Rodriguez, OCD (Washington, D.C.: Institute of Carmelite Studies Publications, 1973), p. 132.

6. N. Cabasilas, *Vita in Christo,* 7, *PG* 150, 685.

7. Cf. J. Kirchmeyer in *DS,* Vol. 6, 853.

8. Dr. Elmer Green, Menninger Foundation, Topeka, Kansas.

9. St. John of the Cross uses the image of fire to describe the suddenness of God's coming and his independence of anything man could do to prepare or to accept such a grace. Cf. "The reason is that if the corporal vision or feeling of the senses has a divine origin it produces its effect in the spirit at the very moment of its perception, without allowing any deliberation about wanting or not wanting it. This is likewise so with the more interior communications since God grants these favors without the individual's own ability and effort, for this is an effect he produces passively in the spirit. The good effect, accordingly, does not depend upon wanting or not wanting the communication. Were fire to come into immediate contact with a person's flesh, that person's desire not to get burned would hardly be helpful, for the fire will produce its effect necessarily. So too with good visions and sensible communications: Even when a person dismisses them, they produce their effect first and foremost in

the soul rather than in the body." *The Ascent of Mount Carmel* Bk. II. 6, in *The Collected Works of St. John of the Cross,* p. 133.

10. St. Nilus, *Sermo Asceticus, PG* 79, 1281D.

11. St. Macarius, *Epistola 11, PG* 34, 412C, 413C.

12. St. Isaac the Syrian, *Directions on Spiritual Training* in *Early Fathers from the Philokalia,* No. 67, (London: Faber & Faber, 1954), p. 202.

13. Diadochus of Photice, *One Hundred Chapters on Spiritual Perfection,* No. 94, trans. D.M. Freeman in "Diadochus of Photice," Vol. 7, No. 4 (1972), p. 348.

14. Ibid. No. 94, p. 349.

15. St. Isaac the Syrian, op. cit. No. 65, p. 200.

16. Ibid. No. 215, p. 249.

17. I. Hausherr, S.J., "Les Orientaux, connaissent-ils les 'nuits' de saint Jean de la Croix?" *Orientalia Christiana Periodica,* Vol. 12 (Rome: 1946), pp. 3-46.

18. St. Isaac the Syrian, op. cit. No. 248, p. 264.

19. Ibid. No. 249, pp. 264-265.

20. Ibid. No. 250, p. 265.

21. Ibid. No. 246, p. 263.

22. On this subject cf. I. Hausherr, S.J., *Direction spirituelle en Orient autrefois,* Orientalia Christiana Analecta Series, No. 144 (Rome: 1955).

23. St. Symeon the New Theologian, *Catecheses,* Sources Chretiennes Series (Paris: Cerf. 1963), Vol. 96, No. 18, pp. 288-290.

24. Evagrius, *To Anatolius: Texts on Active Life* in *Early Fathers from the Philokalia,* No. 19, p. 99.

25. St. John of the Cross, *The Living Flame of Love* in *The Collected Works of St. John of the Cross,* pp. 578-579.

CHAPTER EIGHT

1. Valentine Zander, *St. Seraphim of Sarov* (Crestwood, N.Y.: St. Vladimir's Seminary Press, 1975), p. 91.

2. For a very detailed listing of Greek Fathers who wrote treatises on the Transfiguration cf. Roselyne de Feraudy, *L'Icone de la Transfiguration*

Spiritualite Orientale (Abbaye de Bellefontaine, Begrolles, France: 1978), No. 23; pp. 117-119.

3. St. Gregory of Nyssa, *Commentary on the Canticle of Canticles, PG* 44, 948-949.

4. St. Basil, quoted by Timothy Ware, *The Orthodox Church* (Harmondsworth, Middlesex: Penguin Books, 1963), p. 77. For a theological presentation concerning the uncreated energies cf. G.A. Maloney, S.J., *A Theology of Uncreated Energies* (Milwaukee: Marquette Univ. Press, 1978).

5. St. Gregory Palamas, *Theophanes, PG* 150, 932D.

6. On this dispute cf. John Meyendorff, *A Study of Gregory Palamas,* trans. G. Lawrence (Aylesbury, Bucks: The Faith Press, 1964), pp. 42-62; ibid. *St. Gregory Palamas and Orthodox Spirituality,* trans. Adele Fiske (Crestwood, N.Y.: St. Vladimir's Seminary Press, 1974), pp. 86-129.

7. The text is found in Greek and a French translation is given by John Meyendorff, *Les Triades pour la defense des saints hesychastes Spicilegium sacrum Lovaniense,* No. 29-30 (Louvain: 1959).

8. Ibid. Nos. 1, 3, 38, p. 193.

9. Cf., Lars Thunberg, *Microcosm and Mediator: The Theological Anthropology of Maximus the Confessor* (Copenhagen: Lund, 1965).

10. V. Lossky, *The Mystical Theology of the Eastern Church* (London: James Clarke & Co. Ltd., 1957), p. 111.

11. Cf. G. Maloney, *The Cosmic Christ from Paul to Teilhard* (New York: Sheed & Ward, 1968);
also Robert Faricy, *Teilhard de Chardin's Theology of the Christian in the World* (New York: Sheed & Ward, 1967);
C.F. Mooney, *Teilhard de Chardin and the Mystery of Christ* (New York: Harper, 1966).

12. Nil Sorsky, *Ustav,* p. 28, cited from the critical text of M.A. Borovkova-Maikova, *Nila Sorskago Predanie i Ustav s vsupital' noi stat'ei* in *Pamiatniki drevei mennosti,* No. 179 (St. Petersburg: 1912). Translation my own.
For a detailed work on Nil's spirituality, cf.
G.A. Maloney. S.J., *Russian Hesychasm: The Spirituality of Nil Sorsky* (The Hague: Mouton, 1973).

13. Cf. H. Riesenfeld, *Jesus Transfigured* (Copenhagen: 1947);
J. Tomajean "La fete de la Transfiguration, 6 aout," *L'Orient syrien,* No. 5 (1960), pp. 479-482;
G. Habra, *La Transfiguration selon les Peres grecs* (Paris: 1973);

Petro B.T. Bilaniuk, "A Theological Meditation on the Mystery of Transfiguration," *Diakonia,* Vol. 8, No. 4 (1973), pp. 306-331;
Wayne Teasdale, "The Spiritual Significance of the Transfiguration," *Diakonia,* Vol. 14, No. 3 (1979), pp. 203-212.

14. *Byzantine Daily Worship,* ed. and trans. J. Raya and J. De Vinck (Allendale, N.J.: Alleluia Press, 1969), p. 747.

15. St. Symeon the New Theologian, *Traites Ethiques,* Vol. 129, in Sources Chretiennes Series (Paris, Cerf: 1967), 10, p. 296.

16. St. Athanasius, *Life of Antony* in *Post-Nicene Fathers,* 2nd Series, Vol. 4 (Grand Rapids: 1957), p. 214.

17. St. Maximus the Confessor, quoted by Timothy Ware in *The Orthodox Church,* p. 327.

18. St. Gregory Palamas, Triads 11, 2, 12, cited by Meyendorff in *A Study of Gregory Palamas,* p. 143.

19. *The Way of a Pilgrim,* trans. E. French (London: 1930), p. 105-106.

20. On the theology of icons, cf. St. John Damascene, *On Holy Images,* trans. Mary H. Allies (London: Thomas Baker, 1898);
L. Ouspensky and V. Lossky, *The Meaning of Icons* (Boston: 1952);
Eugene N. Troubetskoi, *Icons: Theology in Color* (Crestwood, N.Y.: St. Vladimir's Seminary Press, 1973);
Paul Evdokimov, *L'Art de l'Icone* (Paris: Desclee de Brouwen, 1970);
C.D. Kalokyris, *The Essence of Orthodox Iconography,* trans. P.A. Chamberas (Brookline, Mass.: Holy Cross School of Theology, 1971).

21. St. John Damascene, *On Holy Images,* PG 94, 1264.

22. Cited by M. Behr-Sigel, *La Priere a Jesus* in Dieu Vivant Series, No. 8 (Paris: Seuil, 1948), p. 87.

23. Pseudo-Macarius, *Spiritual Homilies,* No. 11, trans. G.A. Maloney, S.J. in *Intoxicated with God,* p. 77.

24. St. Symeon the New Theologian, *Hymns of Divine Love,* trans. George A. Maloney, S.J. (Denville, N.J.: Dimension Books, 1975), Hymn 25, pp. 135-136.

25. T.S. Eliot, *Four Quartets* (N.Y.: Harcourt & Brace and Co., 1943), p. 39.